CW00456284

The Passion from Within

ADRIENNE VON SPEYR

The Passion
from Within

~

Translated by
Sister Lucia Wiedenhöver, O.C.D.

IGNATIUS PRESS   SAN FRANCISCO

Title of the German original:
Passion von innen
© 1981 Johannes Verlag, Einsiedeln

Cover by Roxanne Mei Lum

Contents

Foreword

This series of meditations on the Passion of Christ came into being simultaneously with the dictation of the commentary on the Passion in St. Matthew (written 1948, published 1957).[1] While in the latter the meditation followed the Gospel text without a break, there was a clearly marked lingering over particular scenes. The meditations on these scenes form a whole insofar as they are always concerned with the interior aspect of the Passion event, mostly with the interior states and experiences of Christ, sometimes also with those of the disciples or of other persons taking part in the events. Such experiences of the interior states of persons and events were a very special charism given to Adrienne von Speyr, here as in her other works. It is evidently not a question of "empathy" or of psychologizing, but rather a "being admitted", which becomes particularly clear because these in-sights [Ein-*Sichten*] always prove to be important in relation to salvation history (or "theologically"). They do not pander to curiosity but invite to meditation and adoration.

A few of these dictations took place in a state that Adrienne used to call "hell" in connection with her Holy Saturday experiences, a state of total depersonal-

[1] *Passion nach Matthäus* (Einsiedeln: Johannesverlag, 1957)—ED.

ization in which she most often no longer recognized her surroundings, the purpose of which was the objective passing on of some truth or insight. Sometimes the state of concentration on the mystery, on what was shown her, and such depersonalization were in flux.

One notable consequence is the way in which the theme of the body, of bodiliness, of embodiment (of the Word of God), of body sensations, from the institution of the Eucharist to the Cross, is treated in ever new ways. This has nothing to do with the fact that the author was a physician (though she liked to use occasionally images from this sphere). Rather it has to do with the theological mission of taking the bodiliness of the created human being in his relationship to God seriously—for it stands right in the center in the Incarnation, Eucharist, Resurrection. In this she creates a necessary counterbalance to the inclination of Neoplatonic enmity toward the body cultivated throughout the history of Christian mysticism, with very few exceptions (Hildegard!): the more "spiritual" an ecstasy, the higher it is valued. This is not only specifically unchristian but also unbiblical in general, as we can see from the revelatory visions of the Old Testament that find their climax in the Apocalypse of the New Testament. Here we have, at last, the connecting link with early Christian tradition—Irenaeus, Tertullian, Athanagoras.

The meditations follow the events from the room where the Last Supper took place to the way of the

Cross. The suffering on the Cross and the mystery of Holy Saturday are only marginally touched upon here and remain fragmentary. Adrienne has treated of them in detail in other works.

HANS URS VON BALTHASAR

Going Forth into the Passion

In view of the coming Passion, the Son has to part from everything. Not only from the objects he possessed, from the people with whom he lived, from the habits and situations within which he spontaneously moved, but also from the most precious things he has: his mission, his prayer, his work begun but not completed. He has already drawn the finishing line by announcing his suffering and death to his disciples; now he has also to take leave in solitude. He looks at his hands, feels his body: the time of his Incarnation is irrevocably drawing to its end. His limbs will become useless to him in a pain as yet unknown and unimaginable. He loves his body because he has received it from the Father, because his Mother formed it, because he used it to fulfill his mission. Together with his body, his mission is drawing to an end. The instrument of his body is not used up; his coming death cannot be read from it. And since suffering and death are contradictory and absurd in relation to what he has begun, there is no comfort for him in the thought that the breakup taking place now of what he has begun on earth will be completed on another level precisely through the suffering. He has the healthy limbs of a young man, and he feels the irrevocably approaching death as the panic of pure contradiction. It is the same panic felt by a young person to whom it becomes clear that a terminal illness is consuming him. But he is not ill. For a sick man it can be a comfort to know that he bears the seed of death in himself against which the battle is useless: it teaches him physical surrender. The Lord, however, is conscious of the presence in himself of all the forces necessary to continue doing the Father's work on earth. The opposing power of sin that will put him to death is so far still outside of him. It is contradiction, but as superior force. He will be vanquished by it in his earthly reality. That this will be his victory—on a different level, with the Father—his mortal body cannot be aware of.

He has to part from his disciples, and he recognizes how imperfect he leaves them behind. He would have liked to have had many more disciples and to have brought each one of them much farther. It seems to him that it took him all his time to adjust to the level of their imperfection and that he had only just learned how to handle them. Something in his Incarnation was development, a learning process; life experience played a role for him, too; he now feels that he could make more effective use of what he has gained on the way. Not that he has made mistakes so far, but everything seems to him now a mere beginning; he has only laid the foundations. It was a slow process; from now on he would be able to work more swiftly. And it is just at this moment that he has to leave off. The disciples will soon flee; no one will remain. The betrayal is already in preparation; the course of events bringing him to lonely failure is unrolling.

He has to part from his mission. The mission was: to bring the world back to the Father. As man, he knows how divine this mission is. As man, he also knows that it is incomplete. Humanly seen, not even a fragment of the total has been achieved. Had he taken the task too lightly when he was still with God, in the thought of being able as man among men to do what God from heaven could not achieve? Should he have considered more deeply during the thirty long years of contemplation how short the time for action would be afterward? The confinement of human existence now suffocates him in such a way that he no longer knows how constantly he as man had been in touch with the triune God, which also means with himself as God, which means how right therefore everything was that he did in his obedience. The idea of obedience becomes veiled in his consciousness. He sees himself as one to whom the Father had entrusted something great to achieve and who did not succeed in accomplishing it. Just as he can scarcely remember that as man he always did the Father's will and therefore something divine, so can he scarcely imagine now that he will return to heaven as the Incarnate One, and everything human in him will be his forever and at the disposal of the Father and of mankind. Everything that unites him with the Father and the Spirit is clouded over already by the shadow of the darkness of the Cross. Everywhere he hears the sound: "too late." It is rolling toward him, is approaching. Or could he with a last effort prevent its approach? Ward off the end and death until his mission is fulfilled in a better way? It is like a temptation: one could obstruct the divine spirit with the human spirit, demand another period of time that would not pass in vain, for one would use every opportunity with utter devotion. . . .

Taking leave of human bonds. Of his Mother, of the Beloved Disciple, of all these touching people who were attached to him and believed in him, for whom he had worked his miracles, whom he loved with full human affection. The more he gave them, the more he loved them. He loved them with a childlike heart. He does not know what more to say to them now, how to prepare them for the parting, in order to help them to endure it and keep faithfully to his teaching, which at the moment cannot be fully grasped. He cannot reveal himself to them utterly, because he cannot expect counsel from them. What he says to them he says as God. As man, he is more and more reduced to silence because of their incapacity truly to understand him. In between he says his Fiat to the Father, only to be thrown again out of the Fiat into anguish, a super-human kind of anguish, for everything is so fearful in face of the Father and of the sins of the world.

Taking leave of prayer. The uninterrupted communion with the Father begins to break off. Everything recedes now into the light of estrangement. Humanly it is inexplicable how this estrangement could be ordained by the Father, how the Father holds the spirit of the Son of Man in his hands even before he has received it back expressly at the moment of death. All his life long the Son lived on earth in twosomeness and threesomeness with the Father and the Spirit, but now he falls into the lonesomeness of being merely human, that very loneliness from which he wanted to redeem his fellowmen. His desire was to draw all men into this prayer to preserve them from being forsaken. They were to be with the Father in the Spirit. But this is now taken away from the Son. Until now it seemed that each of his human words was immediately taken up by the Father and even received an answer before a petition was uttered. Now he knows that it will be different: he has to ask as never before, inescapably, even if no answer is given. The word comes back sounding hollow. Or at least filled with the full sound of sin that the Son increasingly hears, stirring up anguish in him. All this is waiting outside the door, and the door will open. There are many doors, but whichever he chooses, it leads into the Passion.

Estrangement

The Lord not only takes leave of the things of this world; he begins to see them disappear one by one. His body, his whole humanity become distant to him in a completely new way. This new experience affects first of all, not his prayer and the refreshing vision of the Father, but rather everything he thinks and feels as a human being. He feels John, whom he loves, to be far away, almost unwelcome and a nuisance; for the disciple stands with all the rest "on the other side". He himself stands alone on the side of the Passion. The others —whether believers or not, whether they love him or betray him—are, every one of them, on the other side. He ought to be able to span a human bridge to them, to love them from their side, bring them into union with himself through his suffering, so that there would be two sides no longer but only the one side of the Father, of the New Covenant. The bridge ought to be built now, before the Passion and also as its fruit: then it would be unimportant whether they suffer with him or not, as knowing or not knowing; he would at least be together with them.

But this longing for a bridge belongs already to the beginning of the Passion, in which all bridges are broken up. John, whom the Lord continues to behold with love, whose beloved features he takes in as he

did before, is at the same time completely strange to
him, because in the disciple's world, suffering does not
form the center. Compared to the Lord, he will only
indirectly share in the Passion, so to say, receive some
crumbs from it. In the time to come the Lord will
not be able to feel him near to himself. And this is
his friend, his Beloved Disciple! From his place in the
Passion, the Lord cannot understand the disciple's non-
suffering. If he were still the same as he was before his
Passion began, the Lord would perfectly understand
that John continues to depend on his teaching and in-
struction in order to be with him, and that he himself,
as God and friend, ought to give him all the consideration he stands in need of: sometimes perhaps very
much . . .

This is what the Lord experiences with John, and it
is much worse with the others. He feels much more
estranged from those disciples whose faith only hesi-
tatingly opens the door to love. Yet he suffers from
this estrangement most of all where he least expected
it: in his Mother and in John. The problem of human
estrangement has so far never touched him. He almost
feels like one already buried. As if all the wires connecting his senses with the exterior world were cut. As
if, instead of the supporting air, a vacuum surrounded
him. He gropes but finds nothing to hold on to. He lis-
tens, but in vain: he hears nothing. But his bodily fac-
ulties are not dead; they are perhaps more consciously

awake than before, because he is aware of what service they have rendered him and could still render him if their use had not been interrupted.

Before him lies the prospect of a violent death. But the estrangement that already now drives him out of the world is no less violent. The pain of separation forced on him is abrupt but continues to spread inexorably over everything, even those things of which he had never been conscious and which he had always taken for granted.

And he thinks of his death. There is a natural death in which the body fails from within; perhaps one part after the other ceases to function in an extreme weariness. It is like a temptation to wish for such a death.

In the distress of no longer understanding, he takes refuge in God but immediately comes up against a wall. Not a wall erected by the Father against him, rather a wall that has to do with his human condition; he himself had to erect it; for he clearly feels: it would not be right to seek consolation in God, to lessen his human torment by supernatural means. And of course, at the moment he knows this, the temptation is greatest: there would be no resistance in the Father *himself* if he went to him; as Son he always has access; he would only need to drop his human garment . . . But that would be infidelity. And he would no longer be God, for God cannot be unfaithful. He would no longer be Son, for the Son can do no other than obey the Father;

and for the sake of this obedience, he may not feel the Father now as Father and himself as Son. He is most perfectly obedient by being now only suffering man in his estrangement.

The Lord and His Disciples
before the Passion

The Son has set his face toward the approaching Passion. This Passion must be strong, all-embracing and exhaustive. He is determined to drink the Father's chalice in its entirety. And because the world as a whole is to be redeemed, he wants to carry not only what is manifest sin but also every falling away from the good, every hesitation and resistance. Already before his Passion he takes part of it on himself: instead of being an active agent, he waits and stands ready; instead of seeking an overall perspective, he remains in uncertainty.

When announcing the Passion to his disciples, he does so in the hope of finding allies in them. He hopes they will stand and wait with him and finally carry together with him. Almost as if he as man keeps forgetting that they are part of the fallen world and therefore also inclined to flee from suffering, protect themselves and reject it. That his words, which come out of his communion with the Father and are therefore divine, will fully reach the disciples only after overcoming manifold resistance. So he experiences the shortcomings of the fallen world on all sides long before the Passion begins. It is the disciples with whom he shared his radiant faith who will be the first not to understand the Passion. The lack of understanding he encounters does not come in the first place from manifest sinners but is found first of all in those whose faith should be alive. The disciples show him, not what the holiness of faith is achieving in them, but constantly, in a kind of stupidity, what original sin has made of them: people slow of hearing.

The inability to communicate to them his own attitude toward the approaching Passion deepens his own suffering and makes it more acute. The events take place not only on two levels—here, God in human form; there, the fallen world—but on three: God on one side, the fallen world on the other, and in between the Lord with his whole plan of holiness, which includes the saints with whom he wants to share a life of holiness. This complicates the situation considerably. There is Peter, a saint in the making, developing at his side into a true confessor and pillar of the Church, and he will also deny him. The Lord has to recognize what is his own in this man, even the truly sustaining principle of what is to be his own in the future. Perhaps the most effective power at his disposal: that which turns a sinner into a saint. But how laboriously this essential principle comes to light! Something of it is seen in Peter already before the Passion, but distorted, as in a curved mirror. The disciples are not yet saints, but neither are they still unholy. In their imperfect stature, they nevertheless are the best the Lord was able to achieve before his Passion. And what is true for Peter and the apostles will be true also for the saints to come.

During the Institution
of the Eucharist

It is a breathtaking moment, when the Word that was with God from the beginning and became flesh and incarnated into humanity suddenly becomes again only words, audible words standing by themselves alone. The words are "This is my body." The new and eternal Covenant, the whole of Christianity, everything that has inaugurated it and everything that is still to come, all this recedes into the simple words: "This is my body." To be sure, they are spoken by him who became man among us, and he is saying them to believers who through faith are in some small way prepared for them. But nevertheless, the words stand there completely isolated. And at the moment of their being spoken, they are completely accomplished. They sum up everything. They are spoken by the Lord who now stands "beside" his body. On the right the Lord, on the left the bread, preceded by the Incarnation, followed by dying and death; in the center of it all these words. And for one moment everything else, including the apostasy of the Church, becomes unimportant because there are these words.

And now the Lord himself is startled in the face of these words. He shudders. For these words sum up the whole mission and present it to the Father. The whole of the Passion is already anticipated in these words; all that was and is and will be is gathered into them and receives from this center its ultimate place; all the states of the Passion: its overtaxing weight, its inevitability, its frightening aspect; all is already contained in them. And yet these words are so weightless; nothing at all measured in human terms. A piece of bread and a command to eat it.

This is enormously oppressive. At the moment these words are said, everything is decided. The world receives a new center. The speaker of these words has to experience this incredible transition, which is a sacrifice. He had in the same way experienced the strangeness of the Incarnation. Having become flesh, he now becomes bread. Having become bread, he becomes Church. These three events stand in a line and become comparable. In a becoming, the Son becomes flesh. In an accepting in which the transformation is achieved, he becomes bread. And then he allows the Church to become his body in her own growth: he gives his body to the bread; he *allows* the Church to take his body and become his body. His one body takes three forms: as incarnate, as eucharistic, as ecclesial body.

And precisely now when his remaining on earth becomes almost too difficult, he gives the character of timeless duration to his earthly body. Lying beside him, but containing him totally, this bread has become his body, and the word uttered has been given to the Church, and in distributing the bread to her members, in multiplying his body, the Church will be formed into his body. There is this moment when the Son is strewn out in all directions, in a trinitarian form that he understands as corresponding to God as Unity in Trinity. Now he experiences this trinitarian form in his humanity: here he was himself in the flesh and became bread in a Church that was becoming a body; he became, so to speak, in his reality a food and an idea. . . . All this however essentially at the moment when the Passion begins to engulf him, when he clearly sees that what is demanded overtaxes him—before he loses every overall view in his suffering.

And now we stand beside him as Church and handle the Eucharist. It is for us a festive ceremony that we celebrate occasionally—"not too often", it would not be good. The Lord has said strange words, but he can only have been distributing bread in memory of his flesh. He speaks of the blood of the New Covenant; we believe we know already what he means by this "New Covenant": what we ourselves mean. . . .

If we had faith in him, we would know that *he* is the truth (and not we) and that in him everything is totally different from what we can imagine. Our meaning and understanding fall short of his truth. And so it would become us to be less sure of ourselves in the face of his truth. But now the Lord demands that our understanding rise beyond its limits toward his inscrutability and incomprehensibility. He states that now his time has come. For us, too. He speaks as the owner who decides in which room he is to celebrate the Passover. In our room this time. And what happens? In its course he has announced his imminent death to his disciples. He has also told them that he is waiting with longing for the moment of sharing this meal with them. If he becomes bread that we can eat, does his life end with this meal? And since bread can be produced repeatedly: Does he come to an end when we eat his bread? Is it a symbolic death, or do we perhaps really kill him when we receive him into ourselves? Was all his human life ordered toward this ultimate reality of bread that is being eaten? Is the prophecy of the Passion concerned with this surrender of his life to us in bread? Could it be that this goes so far that through this, his transformation, his whole divinity passes from him over into us? What manner of being is he taking on himself? The most ordinary one as pure bread, or the most extreme and absurd?

It is as if two parties make an agreement of the utmost consequence for the future, in a few words; nothing more is mentioned later concerning the matter. They live separate from each other, but the agreement stands without any human mediation being evident. And when the agreement suddenly comes into force, it comes down unexpectedly as from a blue sky.

Did the Lord place all his power to work in people into this bread? What is then contained in it? Is it perhaps very risky to eat of this bread? What are the consequences? Everything is so deeply veiled because it rests on so few laconic words without any explanations added. The Lord does not seem to count with us ordinary human beings, who like to have some understanding of what is said to them. And if he lives in this bread that I eat, does it unsettle my whole being? And if he is going to suffer for men, for me, can I keep up my personal relationship with him, or will he disappear into ultimate obscurity? Yet I do not have the option of ignoring this bread and relating to him without reference to it.

It is certain that the disciples at this moment do not take the body in the bread as being without effect and power. If they have to believe him this much, they are also convinced that what he gives them contains his qualities. It is the living Lord himself under an incomprehensible form. In the disciples the Church is prefigured, though without yet having any form or interiority; but to her is given this body that she does not yet know how to handle. That is the breathtaking element in this situation: the Lord endows the Church with his central being as the Word, but the Church *comes into being* only through this word.

It is like coded writing. I look for the key, but when I see what it reveals, where it leads me, what the ultimate message really means, the whole matter seems so fantastic that I suddenly lose confidence in my key. But the sentence on which everything rests: "This is my body", is so clear and rounded that it must mean what it says; but in such a surpassing and extravagant way that the very fullness of meaning makes it incomprehensible.

Other words of the Lord seem easier to grasp: that he has come to do the will of the Father. There, too, we cannot exhaust the whole meaning, but it is clear. "This is my body", however, is incomprehensible even in the literal meaning. It provides no clear-cut shape but immediately an open, endless increase. Yet not an increase that could be traced in a line; rather right away there is a gulf, a wall, a break and constant new beginning.

The Passion itself now appears in the same "fantastic" light. It appears as something unreal. Where will he now suffer? In the body we see? In the bread? Will we cause him to suffer by eating him? The Church receives the body of Christ before he suffers the Passion; only afterward will he go and deliver his body up to death. The Church therefore can suffer together with him only because she has already received his body, so that it lives already in her. Had she not received his body beforehand, she would not be able to suffer with him. And if the Lord had suffered first and then instituted the Eucharist, she would not be able to share in his Passion; she would be at once the triumphant Church with the Lord's death lying behind her. The Eucharist would only be the risen body of Christ. But the Church is made up of sinners, so this is impossible.

The Lord could institute this sacrament only during his life before the Cross, and the sacrament of confession and absolution only after the Cross. The eucharistic body gives the Church access to participation in the Cross. The Cross, not as completed fact, but as something lying ahead of me. I cannot suffer for the Lord if he is not already living in me. If I reject his sacrifice, if I do not accept his Communion, I stand outside and cannot suffer for him. He has to institute the Eucharist also before he himself can suffer. He has placed his whole divinity into this bread, so to speak, in order to be able to suffer freely as man. It even looks as if this bread receives and retains his strength increasingly in direct proportion to his increasing impotency. The Church will continue to celebrate his supper after his death; his power is left in these words and outlives the Lord's death. The bread disappears; the faithful have eaten it. But the words remain in their full divine power undiminished and outlast his death; out of this power the Church will be able to make the Lord's body present at any time.

It will be the same body, but inserted into the fruit of the Cross: the redemption, the absolution, the sacrament of reconciliation. But this does not mean that the body is given to us only after the Lord has redeemed us and instituted the sacrament of reconciliation. Rather, he gives his body to the as yet unredeemed in the full strength of his manhood. Very near to the Mount of Olives, of course, where he will no longer know if his suffering will have results, near to the words: "If it is possible, let this chalice pass from me." He gives his body to his disciples beforehand, so that in every case it is already theirs when the night of incomprehension engulfs them together with him; he wants them to have at least the words and the bread as a pledge from him. He will die alone and without consolation, but he wants them to have at least the comfort of his body.

Eucharist and Anguish

With his words "This is my body", the Lord gives a new mode of existence to his humanity. A lasting one that is not diminished by the fact that the Eucharist may not actually be celebrated for a time; for he gives to the Church the act of his *becoming* bread as well as the state of *being* bread. The whole truth of the Eucharist is contained in the words that remain ever actual, whether Mass is celebrated at the moment or not.

Here a particular form of anguish originates for the Lord: he who is now God and man and bread suffers in his being bread a kind of reduction from which only the faith of men can really liberate him. If men really believe in his eucharistic existence, this reduction is a joy for him. But how many will understand it? To the last moment we will have the freedom to accept or reject it. God the Father knows from eternity whether we will accept or reject it. The Son, however, presses forward into being purely man; he foregoes the certain knowledge of our response to leave it free, undetermined by himself. We are not to have the feeling that our freedom is enclosed in his; it would make us unsure, limit our freedom as we can understand it. His existence in the Eucharist, therefore, is somehow undetermined and fills him now with fear.

He will give up his body to his enemies to be crucified. This body is endowed with natural resistance. It is not from the outset delivered as though powerless in utter surrender without the ability to set a limit or draw back, as is his eucharistic body. And the Eucharist must be what it is: this body given without reserve; but that does not decide the question of whether it will be accepted or not. Yet it is given in such completeness only in order to be accepted by us; it is perfect and complete Eucharist only in this acceptance. In receiving the Lord, we promote in our way the return of the Son to the Father, because our faith cooperates in the full accomplishment of his mission. This makes the Lord's mission in the Eucharist tied and dependent. A mission in powerlessness that can be completed and brought to fulfillment only at the good pleasure and through the faith of men.

One could even say: The Incarnation was the possibility of carrying out a mission wholly in the Father—in the world, but always in the divine consciousness of the redemption in progress. The Eucharist is inserted in the center of this mission but forms almost a mission in itself, shared in part by men; they receive the unheard-of gift but are expected to accept it, not only to satisfy their hunger but in an obedience of faith. How far will this faith go?

There is also the anguish of John: the anguish that does not know itself, anguish of love on behalf of love. He sees that the Lord is squandering himself anew; he does not understand how; he sees only that this extravagance points symbolically forward to his death. He is accustomed to his Master's love going far beyond him and always inventing more fantastic ways. He finds it incredible enough that he has been invited at all to share in the whole work. Now he knows that it surpasses everything he could have imagined. Theology had a long time, two thousand years, to make the abrupt and crude aspect of the event acceptable to us. The contemporaries were confronted suddenly with the stark and unprecedented fact: bread is flesh. John feels as if he is admitted into a madness of love forever inaccessible to reason. Until now the Lord's body was to him the guarantor of his spirit; leaning on the Lord's breast, he is receptive to the embodiment of this spirit and feels the Master's love flow over to him from it, feels his whole teaching contained in his body as in a vessel. If he now has to see this body as bread and eat it as such, in order to partake of the body, he feels that the spirit will be transmitted to him in this way. But the whole process presents a new leap in faith, which, however, comes easier to John than to the others because John's faith has already always lived by this surpassing quality of the Lord. In order to receive the spirit of the Lord through his body in the bread in the right way, he needs only to keep hold of his faith, his grace of faith. Until now he has been used to asking the Lord whenever he felt unsure. Now he has to find his answer in being fed by this bread. For he knows too well that the Lord's body is the vessel of his spirit for him to suppose that the Lord would give his body without his spirit.

The Eucharistic
Experience of the Lord

The Lord first of all feels something like a great bodily emptiness; a sudden state of weakness comes over him, as if he had emptied himself of all his strength, of every certain sense of his body, every distinct movement, every coordination between his divinity and his humanity. As if all his strength had now been deposited in the bread. The bread is still foreign to him when he speaks the words: "This is my body." He only feels as if power has gone out of him, as in the miracle wrought for the woman with a hemorrhage, the power of the miracle. But since it is a question of making the bread his body, all his strength has gone into the bread. It is now there in the bread. If a man had suddenly become adult without passing through the stage of childhood, he would not be accustomed to his body and would not be able to use it as he wills. It is similar with the Lord: he stands beside this bread that contains his power, but he is not yet at home in it. There is a moment of transition: he has given his human strength into the bread and exists now himself as in the middle of a question: he has not yet become himself in the bread. He is uncertain how things will continue. He is still supposed to live on as man among his disciples with whom he shares this meal, and he is at the same time in quite a different place (as if one were expected to talk and laugh spontaneously with those around one while being in the "hole"[1], seeming to share with them while being elsewhere. For the Lord, this elsewhere is the bread).

Then there is the opposite experience: a rising of the new eucharistic existence in the Lord's consciousness, comparable in some way to the Resurrection. But this is only in succession to the first experience, in which, parallel to his ultimate experience on the Cross, "into your hands I commend my spirit", he has tasted for a moment the utter overtaxing of his eucharistic state. On the Cross his whole bodily strength will be consumed in his dying; but already now he has set in motion the consumption of his strength by his word and gives his power into this bread. The bread does not suddenly take on an existence of its own so that the Lord would have to adapt himself to it in a second transformation. Rather, the bread is given the Lord's power of being body as an absolute and the power to transmit his spirit as another absolute. The effectiveness of this power in men is relative: the more a man believes and loves, the more effective it becomes. And while the Lord comes alive in the bread, his power returns to him who said the words of consecration. It is a reintegration that is brought to completion when those who believe and love receive him. There is no moment when the Lord's consciousness of his mission and his obedience

---

[1] Adrienne's term for the states of godforsakenness. —ED.

to the Father exists only in the bread without existing in himself as the Word that speaks. Everything that was in him as Word remains in him and returns to him; in the bread it becomes present through the power of the words he has spoken in the eucharistic framework established by him. The bread is not part of his body; it is his whole body and contains his whole spirit—but in the dependence he himself conferred on the bread.

He does not have a double sense of his body (no more than he would have such a double sense in the Father—one in himself and one in the Father). But, —and this is included in the commandment of love of neighbor—knowing that his body is in this bread, there is something like the continuation of his eucharistic body into his incarnational body; and thus he achieves the full identity between the two forms of being body. He is aware of being consumed by the believer: similar to his loss of power after working a miracle, but also as highest satisfaction because, through his bodily obedience, he can bring believers to the Father. The dissolution within us he feels as his effectiveness in us, not as a process of dissolution. It is an experience close to what he has when the Beloved Disciple leans his head on his breast. There is a mystery of the enduring body of the Lord, who does not wish to be free from embodied joy and embodied sorrow as long as the passing world and the Eucharist are in existence.

Eucharist as Admission
into the Lord's Intimacy

The Lord looks on while his disciples eat the eucharistic bread. He is here the first and highest of those sent by God who within their mission have to obey demands in such a way that these can be taken like nourishment according to each one's wish. Already in his Incarnation as a helpless child, the Lord was the one totally delivered up into the hands of men. But in his early years he was protected by his Mother and foster father from being consumed. The human hands that receive him are good hands. They take care of his body so that it grows and develops. At this moment of his being eaten in the Eucharist, he also comes into "good hands", those of people who, like Mary and Joseph, wish to live by his mission. He is delivered over to them, and they want to receive him in order that he may grow and develop in them.

Both forms of surrender, that of being human and that of being bread, are a surrender to being a power among and for men for their growth in faith. Living among them these last few years, teaching and proclaiming the Father's message, showing them his goodness and revealing to them his prayer and relationship with the Father, he constantly communicated to them the substance of his spirit, and people fed on it, and also allowed a lot of it to pass them by. Only a small portion was understood and accepted, a minimum of seeds fell on good soil and brought forth fruit.

Now, in his new form of existence, he has the same bodily experience. He is eaten by men in order to rise in them; but he knows that they will continue to forget and disregard this and will not give him space to take root in them. He is aware in his body how they eat him in the bread, all the while thinking: it tastes as before, it is a mystery of which we understand nothing. They do lots of things that are against him while trying in between to be a bit more like what he would like them to be, but they do not become integrated.

There are a few who love, like John, who hardly dare to receive the bread but to whom it is a surpassing joy to feel the Lord present in themselves; like John, they experience that resting on his breast does not hurt him. After them comes a whole gamut of others down to the indifferent who are glad they do not need to understand much. Only a few grasp that there are things in the Lord's life and in their life with him that are unique even when they are repeated. Every Communion with the Lord is the only one. Every Communion is given in the shadow of the Cross to which the Lord makes his way from the Upper Room. Most of them think: The Cross will come later, just now the Lord is still here. He sees and feels all this. And these thoughts of the disciples awaken in him now a certain impotence of his own. A weakness, a sense of incapacity. Not a localized pain as later on the Cross, but something general, diffuse, reaching to his whole bodily sensitivity. It is an uncertainty, not of the mind, but experienced in his body, an effect, so to speak, rebounding back to him from the recipients. He feels their failure as personally directed against his body. There is no anonymity here, only the immediate impact of their person on his embodied person.

Formerly, in his public life, for example, he felt compassion with their hesitation, their shortcomings, their withdrawal, limited as they were by their weak human nature. Now it is different—and this belongs essentially to his mission: he has to feel each one's failure in his body. Everything in them that is directed against God is now directed against his body. In him lies the strength to overcome their failure; the effort comes from his innermost center. In every Communion, he does not enter into a peripheral relationship with them, but rather, he is engaged with what is most intimate and central to him, there where his most central and intimate relationship with the Father is located. It is there he allows them to communicate; it is there he admits the restlessness of human sin.

And yet it is also joy for him that through him men enter into communion with the Father, that the Father allows him to open his inner being and let them participate in eucharistic communion with the Father: he gives to human beings, not only "the little finger" or a hand or an arm, but the whole and the best. He shares with them the best he has by giving away the best of himself.

Something of the spent energy of the eucharistic body is also retained by the risen body of the Lord. But the surrendered state of his body before the Passion is more easily understood by men than the surrendered state of the risen body. The situation of the Last Supper will better equip them to receive Communion later than the situation of the Resurrection. The Lord's eucharistic surrender is the beginning of his Fiat on the Cross. The eucharistic state endures as experience for the risen Lord. It is something he knows, something belonging to him. It cannot be said that he suffers from it—his Passion ends at Easter—but there is a quality of sensation that remains. And, after all, we continue to offend God through our sins. But the Father is ready to bear with us and forgive us by reason of the Son's perfect surrender.

Body on the Cross
and in the Eucharist:
Begetting and Birth

The Father eternally begets the Son, the Son eternally begets the Church. The mystery of the Father's quality of being ever greater, of never coming to the end of his begetting, is passed on into the Church through the Son. The Church is not only the Son's work but also the Father's because Son and Father have one essence, and the Father is therefore at the Son's disposal for the begetting of the Church. It is the Father's desire, however, that the Church bear the Son's character; he wants to stand behind his Son. So he will beget the Church in no other way except through the Son. That the Church has to be unceasingly begotten has also to do with our sinfulness. The Son has to extinguish unceasingly what in us and in the Church resists the divine begetting.

In everything men do, be it begetting or something else, they make a start. This start is not always clearly evident, because some aspects of their actions appear as a continuation of what is already begun. Yet there is a start, in the act of begetting as much as in every other human act. This starting point should be related to the eternal begetting of the Word and of the Church.

Whenever we start something that is unrelated to the ever-new beginning of the Word and the Church, we act sinfully.

It is sin that sharply shows up the limitations of crea-tureliness. It separates human consciousness from God and isolates it in itself. At the same moment it also sep-arates me from the other human being. It is the Lord who, in suffering for us, takes all our loneliness into his physical and psychic forsakenness on the Cross and graces us in the Eucharist with a new openness of body and soul to God and other men. Between the eucharis-tic body and the body on the Cross there exists this ut-ter contrast: the first is a body of communication, sur-render, openness; the second, the body of loneliness, of gathering up all the finiteness of sin until death. But by becoming the second, the Lord can entrust himself to us as the first. The first is the work of his love for the Father and for us, so that in the second, this work for the Father may become fruitful for us. Through the Eucharist, the double commandment of love becomes possible in a new way.

The first love is love among equals: God was the first to love, Father and Son in the Spirit. And if we are to love God our Creator, we find access to this only through the love of our equals: love of neighbor, be it erotically colored or selfless. But our love of neighbor is genuine love (instead of common interest) only if it includes the love of God and leaves the other free for God. Love of neighbor finds its fulfillment in the love of God, love of God its concretization in love of neighbor.

The bodily element in its finiteness has its place here. On the one hand, it provides the necessary concretization; on the other, the transition to infinity, the place of setting the other free. Both movements become visible in the Lord's body: the crucified body is concretization; the eucharistic body, the opening out and setting free. The crucified body gathers up all sin and makes it visible in the absolute injury to the body, but only after the eucharistic body has been distributed that has taken into itself the total soundness and invulnerability of his body. Both, however, remain deeply related, for it is as if the Lord's new eucharistic existence, which he lives in other bodies, bodies of sinners, delivers him utterly up to sinners, making it possible for him to be injured, mocked, spat upon, scourged and crucified by all sinners.

The Son is with God in the beginning as the Word that is begotten by the Father. He is also at the beginning of the Church that he himself begets, as the original truth of Christian doctrine. He is, at the same time, at the beginning of the Church as the one eucharistically distributed, but the body-form as Eucharist is not in contrast to his spirit-form as word of doctrine. Both forms are a double expression of one reality: that he is the incarnate Word of the Father. The body-form of the Eucharist is in no way deprived of being word. Whoever receives the eucharistic body receives the whole

Christ into himself: the word as well as the body. He can say "the word of Christ is in me" as validly as "the body of Christ is in me." But his word that is in me is also one with the word entrusted to me as creature, through which I am able to speak. In receiving into myself the body of Christ, I may not commit sin with my body, and in receiving the word of Christ, I may not utter a word that contradicts the word of Christ, a word that is not love, that is destructive of Christ's word. If I misuse the word of Christ, the Word that is Christ *loses its eucharistic content*. For Eucharist is always the pouring out of the Lord who as Word of God has a claim to my whole word. As Word of God's love, he has a claim on my word of love of neighbor.

Since the content of doctrine is love, Christian love is contained in the Eucharist. In him who gives himself as bread and also in him who receives it. The doctrine lives essentially, not in the book, but in life. In the life of the Lord and in all that lives by his life in my life. Whoever misuses the word in any way misuses doctrine. And at the same time the Eucharist. All words of Jesus' teaching are an expression of himself; he is the Word, the Word at the beginning, at the origin, in the eternal generation. So his word is the expression of his divine being as Word as well as of his being human and in the flesh; in his teaching he expresses both simultaneously. He is the substantial Word in the Father as much as in the Eucharist.

On the Cross, fruitfulness is achieved through pain.

Every pain on the Cross is a birth pang and returns from the individual aching member of the body into the center of painful giving birth. On the Cross, the Lord does not beget the Church but gives birth to her. Or better: begetting and giving birth fall together. The Lord's begetting is more clearly seen in the invisible Church, the giving birth in the visible. A Christian wants to exhort another: his desire to do so is the begetting; the carrying out of it is the birth. A person wants to pray: kneeling down is the birth, the prayer itself the begetting. Begetting contains all potentiality, birth the action that makes it visible. Only *one* seed matures in the maternal womb. Begetting is inspiration, birth is performance; but the performance is constantly being newly fertilized (as in the case of someone planning a book, who in writing it receives ever-new ideas that he integrates). The parable of the sower shows the sowing and the result.

We grasp the begetting of the Church more easily at the moment when the Son gives up his spirit on the Cross. This handing over is the begetting. The act of begetting is a more spiritual act than that of giving birth, inasmuch as it is left to the free will of the begetter. The words of the Lord on the Cross are acts of begetting, male begetting, each time the Holy Spirit is the great begetter. After giving this Spirit back into the Father's hand, the Son can only give birth. The power of begetting returns from the Son to the Father: it is the Father who now begets with the word of the Son.

The Disciples' Thoughts on the Way
to the Mount of Olives

They go all together to the Mount of Olives. It is late, for it was already evening when they assembled in the Upper Room. They have eaten the paschal meal and, in its course, the mysterious bread that was the Lord's body. And nearly everyone asks himself: Has anything in me been changed? In what way was this meal different from others? There were many things that were not different. It is the custom for the Lord to give thanks, break the bread and distribute it. They had often shared a meal with him, in groups or all together, and there had been similar gestures. It was new that he told them one of them was to betray him. This makes them feel depressed, though nothing has become evident so far. Some are in their thoughts strongly occupied with their attitude toward the betrayer; they feel anger and rage. Will this betrayal lead to the Lord's death? On the other hand, there is the bread they have eaten: Is it perhaps a clever tactic of the Lord, hiding himself, so to say, in bread in order to outwit his persecutors? Is the bread an escape? Does he prevent something in this way? Does the form of bread add something to his body that makes it different from a mortal body? Something that he withdraws from it? If that were the case, he would

have entrusted *me* with a secret; his love would have
sought my protection; I would have been nourished by
his body, but I would then also have rendered a service
to the Lord. And if it is true that power went out from
the Lord's being, from his visible appearance, strengthening his word and his truth in me: How much more
deeply he must have entered into me through this bread
than he did when we stood side by side with him?

And now we are going together to the Mount of
Olives, and each of us carries Christ's body in himself.
Does this make it easier for the Lord? Or, on the contrary, more difficult through us in whom he dwells?
Has a kind of exchange taken place; is this the beginning of his taking our sins on himself? Dying he will
remove our sin, but perhaps in giving us his body, he
has also given us the capacity to receive him in order to
remove the obstacles in us, so that his dying has already
begun, through us?

And this not only through the betrayal of the one but
also through his giving of his body to us all? Is he who
through Communion enters into us and yet still walks
side by side with us aware in himself of the place in us
that was empty and is now filled by himself? Does he
overcome something in us? We know that the body we
have received is alive; it must be alive—does this mean
that he has taken on himself something that was dead
in us, that was not his, to make it a part of his dying?
What will other receptions of Communion be like? Is
it possible to eat his body so continuously that our own

will be replaced by it? Until all our resistance has been consumed? Until everything in us has become totally his? And what would then be our responsibility? Could one leave everything to his body, leave it to him alone to act, or does the reception go so far as to mean that, having received this body in our center, everything else in us has now to surrender to this center?

John has quickly found his solution: I must let the Lord's love act in me. Period. I must stand by him always, all the time knowing that he is in me, and I must become unceasingly what he gives me. I may not even allow the disquieting thought of the betrayal and all that will follow from it to take over in such a way that the effectiveness of Communion is stifled. I must receive everything in the same way as he gives it, I must answer the exact question he asks.

Another disciple also thinks: To accept in the way it is given. But he has already become a quietist. If the Lord wants more, he will say so. If the present level is sufficient, that is allright with me. If his body is really so full of life, it should have the strength to overcome all opposition in me. In John it was an intensely active listening to the word of the Lord. In this other one, a gradual becoming deaf to the word.

Another again has the opinion that his reception of the bread was no more than an act of faith. He has obeyed, has eaten the bread, not resisted the word. He does not stop to examine whether he really believes the *content* of the word. He sees in the Lord's command a test of faith: The Lord wants to find out whether they are ready to accept even something as abstruse as this: this reality they cannot analyze but are nevertheless disposed to accept with a kind of good-naturedness and good will. They have passed the test, and the Lord can take them a step farther. No one can know what he is going to invent next.

There are also some who rather anxiously watch the process of their digestion. As if they had eaten the pit of a fruit that could take root and grow like a tree inside them (children imagine such things at times). They are waiting to see what effect the bread will produce.

Others again are watching for a spiritual effect. They feel they ought to have developed spiritual senses. They do not know how. In a primitive way they circle around contemplation. They are centered on the Lord in themselves.

But he walks beside them and experiences everything that goes on in them. He is more closely bound up with their thoughts than he was formerly.

The Disciples' Failure on the Mount of Olives

I saw the Lord on his way to the Mount of Olives. He is occupied with his disciples; behind them he sees the seventy-two, and behind these the entire number of those who already believe or are on the way to belief. But with every step he knows more clearly: Now the hour comes when I have to answer for my mission to the Father. He faces a parting in order to go to the Father. He has always been advancing toward the Father, but this time, he feels, it is the last time on earth. On the Cross he will enter into complete forsakenness; but now he goes once more to the Father to give an account of all the details of his mission, irrevocably. He is deeply shaken as human being, as the one waiting for the Passion. Shaken on behalf of the Father who has to witness it, shaken also in himself as the one who has to achieve the whole in a way no human being, himself included, has ever surmised. He will have to give an extreme that he is uncertain he possesses.

And there are these eleven—Judas no longer counts —and he has to take them along, introduce them more deeply; and the time is terribly short. He has to place the whole work into their hands for them to continue.

Each of them should be developed further to his best possibility. It is not a matter of indifference how the very first understand everything and take it on. There is the bigger group, the eight, whom he can lead only to a certain threshold. And the smaller one, the three whom he leads farther. It is terribly difficult to move Peter along. To leave him to his sin of sleeping now and denying later. Peter would be less guilty if he had left him behind with the eight. But he cannot spare him. He cannot confine himself to the true lovers only, for the office has already been established. And even love will come to fail now, and also James. He cannot save them from this failure that will make his own suffering more severe.

The foreknowledge of the failure of the Beloved Disciple and of Peter in his office adds an absolutely personal trait to his suffering. In it he *experiences* the failure of all who are close and dear to him, and he receives through it an insight into the abysmal failure of all mankind, which he will bear on the Cross. This apprehension of the much greater burden ahead of him, acute already in the failure of the few, is dreadful. It is like the refusal of those on whom he had counted most. Those most intimately invited reject the invitation: they have other things to do. He begins his Passion; they are at the moment unfocused. Before the solitary meeting with the Father, there is this infinite sadness that has a clear cause and at the same time is incalculable. It is as with a sick man who has an idea of how difficult the operation will be because even the preparations for it are hardly bearable. The knowledge of the failure of the few occasions an infinite sadness and disquiet in the Lord, having neither form nor face. He seems to get wind of all that will happen in the Church and the world until the end of time—he sees the eight he left behind, the three he took with him, looks into their interior, notices their preoccupations: they are dull, they merely know that he is going aside to pray. The three think: We shall have a share in his prayer, perhaps. . . . Dullness is spread over the whole.

And now it grips him from within, and he begins to tremble; it becomes clear that this really is the beginning. He experiences the same reaction as men who are sinners do, the reaction caused by sin in human nature: recoil and anguish. The fear that was intended to be a natural defense against coming suffering, an invitation to flee, lays bare before him a view of the whole Passion. He becomes aware that by the fact of being human has already taken on himself human sin. So far perhaps in the more active sense of confronting and attacking it; the active confrontation precedes the passive bearing; in reverse fashion to what took place in prayer, where he experienced the passive element first: hearing and beholding the Father. But his active defense against sin always had already a passive element: he was burdened with a nature that was affected by the consequences of sin. Now he comes to know this nature's weakness in a new way: the ways and inclinations it has that lead men into sin. He himself had never been tempted to be cowardly, to flee, to lie—but he sees in Peter what it means to follow the inclination to flight, to escape. And to begin with, simply to go to sleep. The Lord experiences this so close by, in those nearest to him, that through them whom he loves, forms and carries he comes to know something in himself that appals him. He had seen many faults in his disciples before this. But then there was still time for improvement. What is going to be done now, since he is going to die?

In the sleeping disciples, the whole fiasco of his mission is symbolized. The Father sees them all: Judas, Peter and the others. ''These are my disciples whom he entrusted to me, my guard of honor!'' And he begins to sink into a no longer knowing, he ceases to count on his suffering as a force that could change the situation; he separates himself from the effectiveness of the Cross in order to keep only its powerlessness. His evident failure with his disciples becomes a proof that the center of the coming Cross will be the failure of his strength, of all his powers. In the face of his sleeping, denying, betraying disciples, the passive element approaches from outside in order to take possession of his soul.

"My Will", "Your Will"

I was just "someone" with neutral and good intentions. But the moment I wanted to put them into practice, they were thwarted. I decide to read this book. I am told, No, not this one, the other one instead. I want to do a particular work. No, first sweep the passage! The No, the will of others, seems to exist only to train me in renunciation. Then I try to want nothing at all, simply to wait. But that, too, is not right. I have to make plans while learning at the same time to be ready to sacrifice them at any moment. And to do or suffer things I do not like, or which I hate, in such a way as if they gave me joy. To accept with supernatural willingness what nature abhors. But at the same time live wholly naturally, to know and possess and be guided by nature in such a way that I plan what is natural and do not lose the natural disinclination, the natural fear of things I afterward have to accept supernaturally. It is not right to suppress nature from the outset in favor of the supernatural; the supernatural is embraced only when it shows itself to be what God wants. "My will" and "Your will" are thus seen as natural will and supernatural will.

The Son's will is of course supernaturally one with the Father's will, but by nature his will is in conformity with human nature and independent according to the law of the Incarnation.

At the beginning he says: "My soul is sorrowful to the point of death." The "soul" embraces here not only what is natural but also the supernatural attitude. But it is so closely united with the body that it trembles together with the body, just as the body trembles with the soul. The words are addressed to the disciples. He speaks to them before speaking to the Father. They see that he is in anguish; he expresses it by his looks and in his words; his whole humanity seems to express only anguish. The Master, seeing farther ahead than the disciples, trembles with fear and communicates what he feels to his disciples. He does not hide his inner state from them (out of pride? shame? or for pedagogical reasons?). He reveals it to them totally: "This is my present situation."

Then he speaks to the Father: "Not my will but yours be done." This setting aside of his own will and preferring the Father's will must not be a form of definite detachment from his human nature, a rejection of the nature into which the Father has sent him. The "not" has to be spoken and felt in correspondence with the word addressed to the disciples: "sorrowful to the point of death".

At this moment Adrienne sees a great number of thwarted human plans, where the supernatural Yes, as painful as it can possibly be, has to be said within the No of nature. For example, a young mother, her child in her arms, for whom she has painfully battled—he is her only joy, she is wholly focused on him—and at this moment she knows that he will die. But not my will, yours be done, even though it makes no sense to her. A young medical student has a very skillful hand that would have made him an excellent surgeon, but he loses it. A priest, converting many people by his preaching, develops a stammer and can never preach again. An infinite number of examples present themselves.

There is also anguish that includes the body: a man acutely ill, writhing in pain; somebody else stirs up in him the hope for a new medicine, how unimaginably happy one would be, if . . . but no, it comes to nothing, one has to endure in anguish and say "Your will be done."

It seems to the Son that the Father's plan itself recedes into darkness. The goal is no longer clearly evident. There is only one certainty: if the Son gives his will back to the Father, then nothing else can happen but the Father's will. This is a ray of light. We have to learn therefore to have a will of our own and then to surrender it. To make plans and while doing so let go of the plan. The ultimate meaning is found, not in the plan, but in the obedience.

The Lord Is Distraught

The disciples are asleep. It is as if they have run out of subject matter for their meditation. They had intended to be awake, but their prayer is half-hearted, their engagement and active cooperation too lukewarm. They are a little disquieted but tell themselves: After having slept over it, we will be able to see more clearly. They choose a natural solution but totally forget that they have a task to fulfill.

A few steps away from them is the Lord: as the human being, as the One sent, as the Son of God. As man, he becomes troubled; it is mounting up to a tempest. He can do nothing but give himself up to this panic, squarely facing the storm. As the one commissioned, he takes care that the disturbance outweighs the consciousness of his mission (like a man who cannot listen to ghost stories at night but asks his friend to tell him such, and the more urgently the more fearful he becomes). The Lord does not work himself up hysterically into something; he is objectively working at his task: he has to lay all certainty and security aside, has to create room in himself for panic. As God, he knows about the panic he suffers as man; the consciousness of his mission is overlaid at times so that the human panic may, so to speak, directly touch his divinity. As God, he robs himself of clear vision; as God, he closes the

door against any hope and consolation, against everything that binds the Son to the Father. For he cannot
surrender his humanity to suffering and remain as God
untouched in the background. He is the indivisible
Son of the Father who has to accomplish his task undi-
videdly. He has to go into the Passion also as the God
who voluntarily lays aside his power, gives himself into
the hands of men "with hands tied". To this state of
helplessness belongs the renunciation of a clear, overall
view, of a sovereign ordering of things within a time
at his disposal; everything is fleeting, momentary; disquiet, panic, always takes place right now. What is this
noise in the darkness? A mouse? Or a house collapsing?
Or the world coming to an end? Every means of taking
stock of the approaching disaster is taken away. And every disaster seems imminent, immediately threatening;
there is no future. All this affects body and soul as a
whole. Is it death that announces itself? Is it an assault?
What is to be done in such a situation to make a con-
tinuance of life possible at all?

The Three Prayers on
the Mount of Olives

The Lord goes three times to pray. The first time he
takes men with him, he arranges them in order—eight
more distant, three nearer—so that they can share in
his first prayer—as if it had not been part of his plan
to go twice more alone. He knows about Peter's denial
to come, but he does not seem to have reckoned with
their falling asleep here and now. The plan was that the
Church should accompany him into his prayer of suffering. In a kind of procession: the people in the background, then the seventy-two, the eight, the three, and
at the head the Lord, who advances to the place where
the New Covenant is to be established, where the wills
of Father and Son are united in the Spirit. The incarnate Son advances to the place where as eternal Son
he has already always been one with the Father. At the
head of the earthly Church, as her embodiment, he advances toward the heavenly Christ in the Father. Not
only to the Father but also to himself as God in heaven
he says, "If it be possible, let this chalice pass from
me"—like a man who has made a big life-decision in
his youth that with the years becomes extremely difficult to maintain, and now he once again talks with the
self that made the decision at the time. The sleeping

disciples and the people behind him represent the dis-
appointments he has gathered in the meantime; as an
experienced human being, he looks toward the coming
destruction.

At the moment he utters his "Your will, not mine",
he receives a new intimation of the divine will. It
streams into him in a new way, strengthens him, con-
firms him: Yes, he will do the Father's will and carry
the Cross. He has arrived at a point of clarity. He does
not really need to go a second time to prayer. But
now he finds his disciples asleep, and this sleep snaps
within him his communion with them. They did not
accompany him after all. He is left alone. And even
when he exhorts them and enjoins on them to watch
and to pray, explaining to them how weak the flesh
is: the bond between him and them has changed, has
loosened. And in going anew into solitude to pray, it
is like a *return* to the Father. He is the naked, forsaken
Son going to the Father still more stripped through
this disappointment. More divested of himself on earth
and in heaven. He goes to the Father as such, who is
the Father from the beginning, the Father of the Old
Covenant. And in assuring this Father again that his
will must be done, he means the age-old will where it
is no longer necessary for the Son to recognize its unity
with his own will. The first time his earthly will had
been brought into conformity with the heavenly will
of Father and Son. Now he encounters the Father's will
in a way that makes it a matter of indifference whether

his own will has ever been in agreement with it. He has become more lonely, more estranged. Unfamiliar. The Son in his prayer knows no longer what this will looks like.

In returning from prayer a second time, it is the Father's creatures he joins. He does not even address them; he seems to be shy of the Father. Perhaps he would influence the Father's creatures by speaking to them. Until now they were his own creatures in his union with the Father. Now they are the Father's creatures, who withdraw almost simultaneously with the Father's withdrawal. The motivation differs in each case, but the effect is the same. . . .

When the Son goes to prayer for the third time, he stands before God the Spirit, who lives in unity with the Father but at this moment is encountered in the foreground while the Father remains in the background. The Son goes to the Spirit, who had carried the Father's seed to earth, in order to tell him that he will do his will and to offer him anew the whole course of his life. The Spirit carries the Father's seed, himself who is the Son, and the Son wants to recognize in him the Father's will and consent to his whole life's journey. The chalice is now not only the Cross; it contains more: the whole existence of the Son from the moment of his Incarnation. Beginning with the Mother's consent. Men have forsaken him; he had withdrawn from them in order to find the will of God alone. But now he meets in the Father and the Spirit, and in the Spirit he encounters them again embraced by his Mother's consent. It is on behalf of a mankind that is inaccessible to him that he says Yes to the Father in the Spirit, but this mankind appears almost sublimated in the Mother's Fiat. He cannot now find access to this mankind; he himself is naked and poor and almost weightless. He is the mission personified; as naked and as weightless as at the time when he was the Father's seed carried by the Spirit.

There is a huge distance between the first and the third prayer. In the first, his will could be shown to him as something personal, his own, that could freely stand in contrast to the will of God. This has now disappeared, because he has submitted everything to the Father and has left everything behind that had already left him. His whole attitude is that of one already crucified, who remains standing or hanging where he had been placed. In this his third Fiat, he has integrated the Church in himself. Before this his Church was visible in these disciples, these offices already established, this ordered company, in this whole plan of the Son to come before the Father on the Mount of Olives together with his own. Now this Church is asleep; she appears to be laid aside as such for the present; she has failed, has failed also as institution through the weakness of her representatives, even in its three appointed witnesses; and no one knows what the others may be doing. The Church is alive now only in the Lord himself. In him she is alert community, salvific institution.

He bears her in himself in such a way that he himself almost becomes anonymous before God the Spirit. There is no more distinction between himself and the Church: it would really belong to the Church to stand before the Spirit in this third prayer in order to beg him to awaken his will in her. But she has failed to such a degree that the Son totally takes on her role. In his own nakedness he covers her. When he falls to the ground to speak to the Father, his body protects the Church from the reproaches of the Spirit that are meant for her but touch only him, and her only through him.

Between the first and third prayer, the second has its place, in which the Son is alone before the Father in such a way so as not to influence the Father. He is here at the origin of his Fiat, so that this prayer becomes the source of the third.

The Kiss of Judas

For Judas the matter is finished. He does not like to think about it; but it lies behind him. The torment of decision is over. His only care now is to see it through. He is so preoccupied with his plans how to carry it out that he has hardly time for disquiet. At the beginning of the meal he is still present and feels secure. But suddenly the Lord convicts him. And while receiving the piece of bread, he sees John leaning against the Lord's breast: this image suggests to him the idea of the kiss. Only now he sees the full contrast between love and betrayal. Only now that he is convicted by the Lord, and convicted within the Communion with the disciple of love, he conceives the plan of using love as a cover for the betrayal.

He, like the others, understood only fragments of the words the Lord had said to them; their heights and depths escaped them. The others allowed the words to resound in them with honest will and faith, intent on understanding more and making something of them real in their lives; they would not willingly choose what goes against them. He, Judas, was conscious all along in the Lord's relationship with his disciples that the Lord was well aware of their failure but looked at it as a failure in strength and insight: their basic attitude was not false; it just kept getting stuck, and the Lord helped them on. The basic attitude was obedience, incomplete, unenlightened, only half-divined, but it was obedience all the same. They want to follow the Lord. They take their measure from him.

In his betrayal Judas will keep to the gesture of following, with the idea that the Lord will see in it only imperfection but not betrayal. When he approaches the Lord, the Lord will receive him anew. Even when seeing him accompanied by an armed band, the Lord will rejoice that the disciple is turning away from betrayal and comes back repentant. Judas no longer reflects on his decision to betray; that lies behind him, and strangely enough, the fact that the Lord sees through him also lies behind him. He does not reckon with it for the future. This shows the extent of his blindness.

Every time the Lord reproved or exhorted the disciples, it was something complete and then finished with. He did not come back to it. So Judas reckons that his having been seen through is also a one-time event and so finished with and that the Lord now expects conversion from him. For Judas is a disciple and belongs to the group. A reprimand from the Lord had never been a final rejection; his grace had always left a door open for improvement. That is why Judas, after the reprimand at table, feels free to continue, free also to pretend that he is returning to love.

When God was seeking for Adam and Eve after their sin, they, too, took on an air of harmlessness, as if they knew of nothing. Judas wants to appear harmless. He had what they did not, a knowledge of the Lord. Judas has an idea how he can be dealt with. His jealousy also plays a role. While the Lord convicts him, John is resting on the Lord's breast. The beloved friend, the pious child who will never betray, claims the Lord's love for himself. Here Judas wants to come in between. By abusing the kiss, he will show his whole hatred to both of them. They will never again be able to kiss each other without feeling his kiss between them. Judas desecrates the signs of love; he wants to desecrate them forever. It is not merely the Lord's death he wants; he wants the extinction of any remembrance of his love and the distinguishing mark of his teaching.

While the Lord is at the Mount of Olives with the disciples, Judas collects his men and makes his last preparations. He seems to have a kind of intimation that it is this night that the Lord's isolation will begin and the disciples' following fail. He has the feeling that the Lord will forgive his disciples once more, "but with me he shall experience in the midst of his forgiving how great my hatred is." In the kiss, love and hatred shall truly meet.

In him there is also something "threefold" this night: first, the rejection of the Son; then the misuse of the Father's creatures whom he withdraws from him and his Son's work in order to make use of them for betrayal; finally the symbolic kiss that he robs of the spirit of love and fills with the spirit of hatred. What completes itself in the Son in three steps as perfect love

completes itself in Judas in three steps as perfect hatred. He does not have the courage to choose the open
form of hatred but hides behind the form of love in
order not to be discovered at once; the hatred shall become evident only in the soldiers coming behind him.
He calculates that, when he approaches the Lord with
gestures of love, the Lord will open himself to his love.
And then, in the midst of love, he will stab him with
his hatred more effectively. He wants the Lord's disappointment to be all the more stark at the moment when
he believes he is receiving back a repentant lover.

The Lord Receives the Kiss

The Lord urges the disciples to get up, for his betrayer is at hand. For him, it is the setting out into the total Passion. With Judas he has already settled accounts. He had told him at supper who he is. When he told him, "Yes, it is you", his task with regard to Judas was accomplished. The people who stand behind Judas are now more important for him. The betrayer's calculating intention of expressing his hatred in a kiss is recognized by the Lord and passed over. His attention is now given to those who allowed themselves to be hired for this arrest. In these people he sees the mass of sinners coming toward him; they become concrete for him when he is taken prisoner and bound. At the moment of betrayal, this betrayal is already distributed among all betrayers; the seduction of the small betrayers by the big ones is now before his eyes. It is like a negative Eucharist: in the same way as the Lord lives in all to whom he gives himself, so Judas now lives in all the accomplices of the betrayal. Judas is now almost no more than the first one of a whole army of betrayers. And who does not belong to them?

That is the beginning of the Cross, for the Cross is the sin of all. From here the mind's eye goes back to the resolve of the Incarnation: The Son had wanted to become man in order to suffer for all. But had his resolve not led to the opposite of what he had intended? Mankind divided in two camps, two movements against each other: the movement of the Lord with his disciples, the seventy-two and behind them the crowd who believe and love, and the movement of Judas with all the betrayers and all who hate. From the perspective of the Passion, the question arises whether it would not have been better for them if they had never met the Lord, if he had never become man.

The kiss of Judas unleashes the real, physical Passion. Anything that is mere theory or symbol comes to an end. The Cross—the two real beams of wood—is lying ready somewhere. Through the betrayal everything becomes concrete, divinely and humanly. It is the experience of one condemned to death: he is led to a cold prison cell; the bed is hard; the food insufficient . . . and he knows: Tomorrow he will die; the whole surrounding atmosphere is introduction to it. Thus the kiss is the death sentence for the Lord, and the cohort that arrests him inaugurates the acts of violence. With the arrest a new reality is set in motion. At first the condemned had freely appeared before the judgment seat—so the Lord can still ordain: "Let these go free." After that his fate unrolls.

There are a thousand things in life that a man enjoys without reflecting; they do not call for attention. Suddenly these things can be taken away and replaced by other, disagreeable ones. One enters a hostile world. In the same way, the Lord now leaves "the communion of saints" and enters the "communion of adversaries" headed by Judas. But when Judas encounters the Lord, he immediately vanishes into the numberless mass of betrayers.

Judas' Communion

By his betrayal Judas has excluded himself from communion with the Lord. He becomes still poorer by rejecting not only the Lord but also the community. Though the rest of the disciples give now a pitiful impression with their denials and their flight, the Lord nevertheless lives in them, and they are somehow on his side in spite of everything. The Lord feels in himself that he is in communion with them. The disciples are unaware that in every Communion they also contribute a share to the miracle. The miracle that the Lord implants in them is at the same time a miracle they obtain in the Lord. The miracle of that faith that moves mountains through them in the Lord. The miracle draws strength also from them. They are for the Lord what the Lord was for the woman with the issue of blood who touched him. A power goes out from them into the Lord. Even though this power can scarcely be a real, positive factor.

When a Christian receives Communion, an intimate relationship is formed between him and the Lord: the Lord lives in him, something of him lives in the Lord. But no one communicates privately; the Church communicates in him. Something new of the Lord begins to live in the Church, and something of the Church lives newly in him. And at the same time: when a person communicates and the Lord gives and receives in him communion with the Church, something of this comes alive in every fellow communicant, even every fellow believer. With every individual Communion, a strong pulsation goes through the communion of saints to the Lord and returns from him again.

When a person separates himself from the Church, therefore, there are unforeseeable consequences. Judas' Communion was not only an "unworthy Communion", it was a desecration, a sacrilege, because he rejected faith in Christ's presence in the bread, faith in the power of his love. Exteriorly receiving like the others, he rejects what he receives. The miracle of the Eucharist consists not only in the transformation of the bread but also in the Lord's giving the recipient a faith enabling him to receive him. A faith that submits to the word of the Eucharist. Judas' betrayal, however, kills the miracle of the word in himself. It is not true to say that nothing happened when he received. The fact is that what would take place in the immeasurable grace of union if he had faith now takes place in the immeasurable estrangement of evil.

Judas and Apostasy

There is a very great difference between a sin committed in momentary weakness and the sin of deliberately
turning away. When it is a sin of weakness, there is
grace like a safety net, catching the sinner: he cannot
fall lower. So it was with Peter. Judas however turns
away. The two scenes, each by itself, are close together.
Peter's denial is foretold after Judas has betrayed but before the kiss. The weakness of the Church appears built
into the story of betrayal, and so a glaring light falls on
it. If there had been no Judas, Peter would be the great
betrayer. It is only because he stands in the framework
of a still greater betrayal that we find a thousand excuses for him and for the faults of the Church continuing and occurring over and over again.

The image of the Church will always show everything side by side: the Lord with his grace, those who
accept grace, others who somehow oppose it, others
who momentarily reject the acceptance, and finally
those who fall away completely. Apostasy belongs to
the Church as much as do the saints. She is constantly
shaken about as in a basket, until in the end she has to
do with everything that lies between these extremes,
the perfectly good and the irredeemably evil, and all
the different shades in between.

And yet the whole is always contained in the whole:

the whole Church experiences everything from one
extreme to the other. Every individual Christian has
a sensorium for the whole gamut, feels through the
whole, bears in himself an image of the whole. When
Aloysius who was so utterly protected feels nauseated
by immodest conversations, it shows that he has a sense
of what is bad. He has a very refined sense. There is
hardly a saint to be found in the Church who from
a neutral center has experience and knowledge only
of what is good, who would not only reject evil but
also be ignorant of it. Hence the importance for us to
know that in the Passion everything is present and has
its place. The Lord integrates in himself the Church
as she is. He carries the Church eye to eye with her
apostasy: where she ceases to be Church, refuses to
be Church. In the confrontation with Judas, he carries everything including the excommunication. And
of course also Peter's denial to come. He carries everything heaven will have to carry later. Hell therefore is
never more itself than at this moment of confrontation:
for hell is what the suffering Lord cannot take upon
himself. The sin of Judas—and of all apostates—is carried on the Cross in a somehow preliminary fashion.
But when, after the Cross, the Lord passes through hell,
this comes to meet him as a new, amazing gift from the
Father. Something of it has already stolen into his Cross
without one's knowing how or when. Judas nails the
Lord to the Cross; he approaches the Lord from outside, so that he cannot be at the same time assumed

into his suffering. The Lord did not come to bear his own betrayal, the betrayal of which he is the victim. There are various ways in which sin can be related to the Lord's suffering: some sins are directly taken up and borne along; others can only be atoned for indirectly, since the sinner, on the one hand, wants the crucifixion and, on the other, does not want to be redeemed. The case of Judas can be put right only beyond the Cross in hell (as something that was hidden in the Cross).

There is an intensification of negative force at work in the apostate. He resembles a man who works swiftly and surely to erect a wall in order to make the Lord's image, which he knows exactly, disappear and become unrecognizable behind it. Every breathing space he might allow himself could offer grace an opportunity to catch up with him. At the moment of turning away, when he is perhaps still hesitant, he could still be touched by grace, but he braces himself against it and demolishes all the arguments of grace that could still persuade him, for at the beginning grace is still quicker than apostasy. He concentrates all his powers on resisting and destroying them. This he does, not merely in a gesture of postponing and brushing away, but he builds a wall with the will to paint a new image on it, knowing all the while that this image will last only if he keeps on maintaining and strengthening the wall with an utmost expenditure of strength and output. This fortification quickly becomes bigger than the terrain to be defended, and to such a degree that the final bastions no longer have anything to do with the original plan, the actual turning away from God. It often results in an anti-God bulwark, in which the anti-God image bears no resemblance to the primary image of God; no comparison at all is possible. The negative keys no longer mirror the positive qualities of God. Everything is totally distorted. Such a man might say, for example, "I do not recognize the freedom God gives me as freedom, I see it as unfreedom. I imagine freedom to be like this . . ." And then he might make a statement that an unprejudiced observer would still believe to be able to see as a negative contrast to the rejected opinion. But the plan to apostatize has to be carried out so quickly that the apostate has always already arrived elsewhere. The rejection of God remains, but it already has a new face. The apostate is somehow multiplied by the devil into many apostates. Perhaps he intended to put some construction of his intelligence in the place of God. But his intelligence does not work quickly enough for what he aims to do; he has to invest more: his strength and time, his bones and blood, his heart and soul, his manual skill and his arithmetic talent, every gift he possesses. He has to allow himself to be divided up into these, to convince himself through these, and grant to each the primacy over the others. Apostasy is absolute fragmentation, the opposite of the unification in the Church and in the Lord brought about by faith. At first the apostate is like a member in the body of the Church that begins to hurt because it wants to make itself separate; when it has fallen away from the body, it disintegrates further and further into its component parts. Apostasy is the sin that forever generates new sin. Its time is never now but already just past. Every possibility of arrival at completion is already cut off by a contrary construction.[1] One could also express it the other way round: every sin that goes on generating sin in this way is an aspect of apostasy. The possibility of apostasy lies in every sin. There is a kind of determination to sin that can with unbelievable speed turn into apostasy.

Apostasy is a mystery of disintegration, affecting consciousness itself. Consciousness, then, is like a pregnant animal, let us say, a cat that suddenly and unexpectedly bursts open and produces seven kittens. Is consciousness now seated in one of these seven or in all of them,

---

[1] The time of sin is disintegrating time. The ever now, the true moment, is a time that creates space, that allows us to have time to do, to consider and possess what one ought to do, consider, possess. Good time is time as gift, time that adds up. The sinner, however, "has no time". While I am sinning, my sin is already fixated, its becoming is arrested and past. I can borrow from my good time in order to look forward to sin and picture it to myself. In apostasy, this, too, is impossible; there is no approach to sin, only an always coming too late and the necessity of surpassing what went before. The eternal time of perfect faith is a time of making space for God and receiving space from God. The time of apostasy is the time of pure unbelief in which everything present or future is always situated already in a past. The greed in apostasy gulps up everything that is enduring and becoming and puts it behind itself. This is not the case in ordinary sin; one remains accessible to counterarguments and does not cut oneself off from faith.

or in their claws, their colors, or the burst belly of the mother animal? This is an image of the speed with which sin is generated from sin.

To do good is always an effort for man. In evil he is, on the contrary, at once everywhere at home. He never comes to a complete learning about what is good, but evil he knows already. But the total discomfort remains with him, especially if he has known the perfect good, the Lord, as the apostate has. It can hardly be envisaged how the apostate could stop the disintegrating movement and turn back. Perhaps Judas did well when he took his own life, because in time he would have moved ever farther away.

The Role of Money in the Passion

In itself money is colorless. In the mind of the high priests, it can be sacred insofar as temple treasure can be used to procure things for the glory of God. But this "sacred" money is now being used to pay for Judas' betrayal; it is blood money. It is desecrated and utterly devalued, so much so that when Judas brings it back and throws it into the temple, it can no longer be used for a sacred purpose. It marks the sum, the price for which the Son of God was sold.

The Church has to pay attention to these widely differing evaluations of what in itself is neutral. After all, the Lord purified the temple of God with the whip and drove the money transactions out of it. That does not mean that the Lord attacked the temple treasury. Insofar as spiritual interests are materialized in money, there exists a certain point of comparison with the Incarnation. The Church is not only concerned with men's spirit; man is a composite of body and soul, and the Church herself as visible institution is bound up with material necessities. It is her task to try and achieve a balance between the spiritual and bodily interests of men. For example in marriage, but also in confession, where often material things are at stake. But the Church may not onesidedly concern herself with what is material. For she belongs to the Lord.

The Lord became flesh to make himself better understood. Coming from God who is spirit, he became God in the flesh, who, however, as the one who is to rise from the dead, unceasingly strives back to the Father in the Holy Spirit, making us participate in this striving. What the Church brings about in men ought therefore to be an illustration of what the Lord has destined them for. He himself had a purse, and his disciples handled money; they bought and paid. Bodily wants could only be met by means of money. But all took place in the service of the Lord's mission and, finally, at the Father's service. The incarnate Son thus has shown us that money can be used in a spiritually meaningful way. He did not attack the temple treasury, but he himself paid the temple tax.

But at the same time he was intent on pointing out the dangers of money. Money is mammon and cannot be served simultaneously with God. Whoever does so, the rich man, cannot pass through the eye of the needle. But it is only during the Passion that he gives the great lesson: He himself is sold and valued for money, and this money comes from the "sacred" temple treasury. Here the believer, the Church, must pay attention.

Taking the Church
Back into Himself

There are always two tendencies in the Church: one toward union with the Lord—the effect of the grace from the Cross—and one toward falling back and disintegration. The Father eternally generates the Son. In the same way the Son unceasingly generates his Church, because she is whole only in him, having in herself the inclination to move away from him. The Lord has to draw her to himself constantly in a new way, so that she does not move away from the place of her generation, the Cross.

Now when approaching the Cross, the Son draws the Church wholly into himself. She is already in existence in an imperfect sense. He takes what seemed to stand beside him momentarily back into himself in order to generate it once and always from the Cross.

This taking her back into himself keeps the Lord's office alive. He alone is the High Priest on the Cross through whom everything that is official in the Church can receive life and bear fruit. Not in the sense that he takes away from his priests the office entrusted to them. But this taking back is the condition that allows the office to be conferred and to be exercised in a living actuality from the Cross. Every priest in the Church has to be constantly ready to allow the Lord to work through him, to keep his office at the Lord's disposal. As eternal High Priest, the Lord will also fill the official actions of his priests constantly from the Cross. It is a fruitful exchange.

Some aspects of the Lord's relationship to the Church can be explained only through the example of the marital relationship. The man gives to the woman the seed he has gathered together with her in view. He has also in some way taken it from a woman, for he is born of woman. This is especially true of Mary, who is first mother and then bride. She forms the incarnate Son from her organs, and what he has received from her he passes on to the Church in his disciples. It is also possible that the man who phantasizes about the woman to whom he will soon give his seed has more seed to give than he would have if he had not been occupied with her, so that the woman helps him to form his seed. The Lord also is much occupied with his Church and with the manner in which she is to be made fruitful; and the manifold weaknesses of his disciples increase the Lord's receptivity for the Cross.

In some distant way, one could also recall the word: Of him who receives little, little is expected, but he to whom much has been given is expected and enabled to bear much fruit.

The Church is now personified in Peter: it is he who adds much to the Cross of the Lord through his imperfection, his know-it-all attitude, his ever-repeated missing of the point and falling short. Thus a heightened fruitfulness is demanded from the Lord. But since he embodies the bride, he has to conform to the open receptiveness of the bride. The bride leaves herself, her wishes and girlish dreams to the bridegroom, for him to come and bring her life to maturity and fruitfulness. *How* he does so should be all the same to her, even though it may not correspond to her romantic ideas. The Church in Peter, too, should be ready to accept fulfillment from the Lord as he thinks best. Peter must not take the sword in order to enforce his own immature dreams of a kingdom of the Church on earth.

The young girl who becomes engaged may talk of her bridegroom and of her own thoughts and desires. But it is not hers to take the initiative. The bridegroom sees perhaps that she is not fully mature and will receive only in marriage her full potential to become wife and mother. But precisely as a lover, though still an inadequate one, she understands that she must not be the leader in love but needs to be led. The bridegroom begs her: Leave everything to me; he cannot tolerate the fact, therefore, that she keeps proposing new things of her own invention and forces her own well-meant ideas on him. Much in her proposals may not be without good sense, but at the moment it is more important that she learn to leave herself to him. So also the representative of the bride-Church: Peter with his proposals and, finally, his sword. It is not bad that he draws it; the intention is good. But he is not acting according

to the intentions of the Bridegroom. Much of what
the Church does need not be objectively wrong. But it
is subjectively a fault because she thinks, resolves and
disposes on her own impulse.

At Communion the Lord receives his disciples into
himself as they are: with all their weaknesses, and he
enters into a personal relationship with each. But they
are all together at the same time the Church. So the
Lord suffers in the Passion not only for individuals insofar as they are sinners but also for the weaknesses of
his Church as a whole. For the Church whom he has
taken back into himself after she had already come into
existence in his disciples. Now she is to receive her life
from him in a definite way. By taking her back into
himself, his capacity for suffering is enlarged and, with
it, his fruitfulness.

The time of the Lord's betrothal to the Church lasts
for the three years of his converse with his disciples.
The marriage takes place on the Cross and in the Resurrection. In dealing with his disciples, the Lord also
receives inspirations from them, just as the bridegroom
takes into consideration suggestions made by the still
immature bride while all the same keeping control.
In the final form given by the bridegroom, the bride
will no longer recognize what comes from her but will
receive everything from him. When Peter meets the
Lord again after the Cross and is definitely appointed
to be shepherd of the lambs, he will no longer recog-

nize his own suggestions in the office entrusted to him, not even his betrayals and sword incidents, but only the pure gift of the Lord—though much of this gift will *rest* on the fact that he has once betrayed, that he wanted to be washed all over, that he drew the sword, that he went fishing with his companions without catching anything, until the Lord came. . . . When the Lord brings something about, he does not use positive suggestions; rather he reveals weaknesses. For in his eternal conversation with the Church, in forming her, he cannot only take note of what he himself wants but has to adapt himself to the situation caused in the Church by men's failures. There is an everlasting and living relationship between the absolute of God and our human failure, which somehow receives through the office a framework and support, an unfailing possibility to rise up to the Lord.

The Church is the mysterious entity mediating between the Lord's idea of her and the reality as which she appears in the world. In the Lord she is the perfectly pure bride designed by him, whom he tries to make a reality; in the world this bride can often give the impression of being a harlot. She is the image before one's eyes and also the image living within us. A man looks at another and then thinks of him with closed eyes: he carries a picture of the other in his memory that will differ slightly from the reality. But he nevertheless has to close his eyes and carry the picture in himself if he wants to come close to what it depicts. The Lord keeps his eyes closed in the same way, while seeing Peter and drawing him into his own purity and his own obedience.

The Flight of the Disciples

All of them flee simultaneously, but each one by himself, not like sheep that scatter when the shepherd is
slain, not one following after the other. There is no
leadership and no following in this flight. Each one
flees in the suddenness of a spontaneous decision. If
there had been different ways and directions, each one
would have gone his own way. The truth of their communion lies only in the Lord. All the bonds that unite
them to each other deep down pass through the center
of the Lord. None of them can be determined by the
other; all are, in a genuine spiritual and religious sense,
determined by the Lord as their superior. Though they
are not conscious of this, they have each learned during
the years to deal with each other in their union with
the Lord.

Peter is still full of the words he himself invented,
the assurances he was the first to offer the Lord. They
were addressed not only to the beloved Master but also
to the Lord of miracles, of victories, who until now
had always found a way to get out of every difficulty.
Now that the Lord plainly does not *want* this anymore
but manifests the desire to suffer, which conflicts with
the will to victory as Peter understands it, Peter finds
himself in a perplexed state that prevents him for the
moment from continuing to follow the Lord. His flight

implies a certain personal rejection of the Lord, but not without a hesitating acceptance that is somehow physical. Peter here again embodies something of the Church as bride. Between him and the Lord there exists a bond and an attraction; already during the flight he resolves to look anew after the Lord. Fleeing, he steps on the way the Lord has gone. In spirit he has said No to him; in body he follows him from a distance. He resembles a pregnant girl having a bodily connection with a man that others do not have. The office he has received is something physical that is somehow independent of his attitude of spirit.

John made his decision with the same haste as the others; with him it is a sort of panic of love. He cannot bear to see the Lord treated in this way. He cannot bear his Passion; nor can he bear *himself* in the framework of this Passion of the Lord. He had the deepest faith that his bond with the Lord was something valid forever. And he was equally sure that it meant the same to the Lord. Now he sees that the Lord willingly allows himself to be taken prisoner, for he says, "Let us go." According to his own word, the Lord places himself under the law of the fulfillment of prophecy. All human connections of love and surrender appear thereby crossed and broken. The flight of John is an explosion of powerlessness; had it taken place less suddenly, motives could have been found: "It will be easier to bear when one is absent and does not see everything; one's pain will not burden the Lord still more", but it happens too quickly for real reasoning; it is like a stroke of love, like a sudden fire immediately causing a conflagration. His love is for the Lord and for himself: "Not to be here where I am!" He is driven away so quickly that he is unaware of the betrayal. His imagination does not register what it is that he is doing to the Lord, that he, even he, is fleeing. He is totally unprepared; never for a moment did he consider the possibility of something like this happening, and when repeating his assurances after Peter, he was convinced of remaining faithful. Suffering, death and resurrection he saw as purely symbolic expressions. He is so accustomed to being always shown by the Lord the continuation of everything into heaven to the Father that it is impossible for him to imagine that the whole could suddenly end in tragedy.

Thomas flees because he sees no other way; but even during the flight he considers the return. He is unsure: Would it have been better to stay? Or to flee even farther away? Or to return? He remains in the dilemma between belief and unbelief, reflection and disinclination to reflect, and being thrown back again . . . from thought to thought. He is perhaps the one most given to reflection during these moments. And yet he removes himself farther and farther away. While asking himself if it would be more intelligent to return, he keeps on running. Not in order to remain true to his decision to flee, but in a mounting confusion, a growing need to reach a clarity valid for himself.

They scatter like a gathering that is dissolved because no one knows what to do next. No decisions have been made as to where to meet next, how to continue, even about an orderly parting. The question of the following remains unfinished and open . . .

Practical reflections do not play a role for any of them. They all have the impression that they have witnessed a clear and unexpected denial of divinity by the Son of Man, a divinity that nonetheless had proved itself as certain. The Lord goes into suffering that he wants to endure as a perfectly human suffering. That is for them all like an opportunity offered to them for dismissing much of what they had divined as supernatural. They are very human in their flight and try to see the God-man himself as an ordinary human being: their flight is human reaction to the human fate happening to a fellow human being. The Lord himself renounced his divinity, so they also renounce their faith in the Master whose powers reach into the life beyond. He conceals his divinity, and they feel that therefore they, too, need no longer take account of it.

At the Trial

There is a certain sense of relief in being led to judgment: the situation is already so bad that nothing can make it worse. From the interrogation now beginning, the Son of God will emerge vanquished in any case. He does not see the questions asked as a chance for himself; his whole attention is given to the fact that he is permitted to bear witness to the Father even there where it is not accepted. It is not even urgent at the moment that he suffer, because he cannot convert Caiaphas and those like him in any case; he experiences a joy in the midst of suffering and its total hopelessness, because he can once more give testimony to the Father. A joy in going beyond, in doing more than is exacted, and speaking words destined only for the Father's ears.

But when the interrogation begins and he looks at the people confronting him, he feels as if he prefers the armed men of a little while ago. It was less disquieting to be delivered up to brutal force than to this milieu of mendacious minds. The wretchedness of his situation becomes more poignant. Before this, in the joy of bearing a pointless witness, the Father was the one who counted. Now these men are in charge. These are the men who insist that they are defending the Father against him. And they are the ones who had the special task of accepting the Son as the one sent by the Father.

They ought to embody the Father's kingdom on earth and form the basis for the Church to be founded by the Son. But all they present is an image distorted to such a degree as to be unrecognizable. For the Lord, the word is confirmed that new wine cannot be put into old wineskins.

Now the deeper dimensions of the Passion open up: from the ignominy heaped on himself as the one sent by the Father to the pain he suffers on the Father's behalf that those who here speak in his name are so full of malice and look for nothing but themselves, which they camouflage with the Father's name, finally to the pain he sees the Father suffer for the sake of the Son who took on himself this failed expedition of the Incarnation. He also sees the impression the flight of the disciples leaves on Caiaphas' mind; it is as if he were condemned to see the disaster constantly through the eyes of others, called to submerge his own suffering in that of others: the Father's, the disciples', that of mankind in general. For he sees sinners now more as sufferers. And on account of his isolation, he experiences as imposed on him an increased difficulty in communicating himself and sharing himself with his own and with those in whom he had placed his hope. He does not suffer from his isolation for his own sake; he suffers from it *in them*.

~

As God, the Son is always aware of the Father's perfect power. But now when speaking about this power before his judges, he chooses to see it from his standpoint as the captive prisoner: he attributes to it particularly what is lacking to himself. The Father's power was visible for him always in the fact that he is surrounded in heaven by believing, loving and praising creatures. He, the Son, is now surrounded by unbelief and an absence of love. Being thus despoiled, joy springs up in him because the Father in heaven has all power. But as soon as this joy arises, the harshness of unbelief around him strikes him with greater force. From the thought of the Father's power, he is more abruptly thrown down into the experience of his own powerlessness, which the Father chose for him. His human destiny would hit him less had he not known the divine. And there exists no hope that the power of God might spare him the Cross. So his suffering is more bitter than that of one who keeps a ray of hope alive that the interrogation might take a more favorable turn. Nothing is more irrefutably clear to him than his own powerlessness. He speaks of the Father's power as a sick man would speak of health.

Then there is also the thought that the power of God would be mighty enough to change all these unbelievers into believers. But God is so powerful that he cannot be deflected from his plan that the prophecies must be fulfilled. The Father's power must be exceedingly strong for him to look on powerlessly when the

Son goes into the Passion—as if someone who had the power to raise a dead person to life would prefer to let the beloved friend die in order to bring him back, instead of preserving him from death. Such an attitude witnesses to unbelievable superiority.

Peter's Denial

The Lord on his way to the Cross takes the Church with him in himself. But there is something in this Church that is alive in Peter and that finds its first opportunity of showing itself during the Passion. This something would have enabled Peter to be concerned about the Lord's well-being in virtue of his office and his love; it would have helped him to keep up a certain rapport between the Church and the suffering Lord all through the Passion. The intention with which he follows the Lord into the house of the high priest is at first good. It reveals his sense of responsibility. But the good beginning is not followed up; he breaks off before the decisive step has been taken. In no way did Peter come in order to deny. He wants to help in whatever way he can. But as soon as he senses danger for himself, his own safety becomes more important for him than the Lord.

He loses contact with the Lord at the moment when the Lord cannot do anything for him because he is bound. Peter does not yet possess the Lord's presence in his prayer. The Lord is, in body, separated from his disciples; in addition they suddenly realize that he might die like any human being. They had not reckoned with this. They grasp this death at a late hour, the Resurrection even later, though the Lord had foretold both. They operate like blind men with their own limited ideas and put their own hopes in the Lord's place.

The Church as Peter imagines her is a kind of organization. He looks ahead: the Lord will be the leader; there will be members, they, the disciples, in the first place, each integrated in relation to the others. He sees all this in an earthly dimension. That the leading position of the Lord and the role of membership could belong to the supernatural order does not enter his thoughts. And now that the Lord is taken prisoner— in Peter's view, almost lost—he has the feeling that he must bring himself into safety. He means this in an *ecclesial sense,* even though it is a mistaken one. He is conscious of the ecclesial office particularly entrusted to him; in a completely earthly way: just as anyone who has received a clear-cut task. He does not see the Church as a (supernatural) whole, does not understand that he draws the whole Church with himself into the denial. All he sees is the concrete advantages the denial would bring him personally in the world, and perhaps also to one or other of the disciples. They will somehow be able to remain together and survive this disastrous time and so on. With everyone who can save himself, another part of the organization can be saved, and so on. Peter does not understand that he is no longer a private person. He resembles Adam in this: Adam implicated the whole of mankind, and Peter the Church. Adam set mankind against God the Father; Peter sets the Church against the Son. Here begins the whole fearfulness of the Church when confronted with the world. As God, the Father leaves humanity the freedom to turn away, so the Son the Church, though it is men, sinners, who hold the Son captive. But both times it is a question of leaving them free on principle. As long as they remain in God, the divine power is sufficient to keep them on God's way. So there is a parallel now between the Father's disappointment with his world and the Son's suffering on account of his Church. The suffering from his Church is for him like the most acute form of suffering from creation. He cannot suffer it in a general way in order to bring it back to the Father; he has to suffer in addition from his own creation, the Church; otherwise he would in a way take on the Father's suffering instead of his own. He might somehow distance himself from his own body. And he needs to have his own suffering also because he will remain in the Church as in his body. If he had no suffering to bear from his Church (if she were, for example, completely holy), he could almost reproach the Father for a fault in his creation: if the Father had created a Church straightaway, mankind might never have fallen into sin. But now the Son's Church is still more fragile and precarious than the Father's creation. Suffering from his Church, the Son gathers together the sinfulness of the Father's creation.

∿

The disciples learned to pray by living with the Son. They adore the Father and present their petitions to him. And they receive much of what they ask for— through the Son. They understand both: that the Father grants them graces and gifts, and that on earth the Son shows them the way. But he is for them, above all, the Master, the leader, the superior, and in no way God's only begotten Son. The Lord is for them that special man who has a unique access to God. And he certainly came to them from God, but they see, above all, this section of his way, and not his way from the world to the Father. It would not occur to them to pray to him —least of all would it occur to Peter during the Lord's arrest. That he could be adored remains outside their comprehension. Christian prayer has not yet found its form during the Passion; it will do so only with the Resurrection and Ascension. The time in between is used to prepare this prayer; Pentecost only brings the true Spirit of prayer, the ultimate understanding.

So the Church does not pay attention to the Son's divinity during the Passion. She places him on her own level. She understands herself as an earthly reality and sees in the Lord her head, a kind of foreman, like the master in a workshop. In his denial, Peter does not pay attention to that side of the Church that is part of the Lord's mystery, the mystical Church. In this sense, the reality of the Church has not yet found its form either. It is still hidden in the Lord. The disciples see in some way that the Lord carries both, prayer and the Church, in himself. But he does so as the favored one who entertains special relations with the Father. What they miss altogether, with regard to prayer and the Church, is the dimension of the Holy Spirit.

The besetting sin of the Church in Peter's following is the need to be self-sufficient, to erect scaffolding everywhere, to draw lines that are easy for her to see, to overrate hierarchies and such. Much is done by the hierarchy for its own sake and not for the sake of the Lord. No one is more forgotten in the Church than the Lord. The pope attracts far more attention, because he is visibly alive and active.

God gave a body to man and also to the Church. The body of the Church is her visibility. And man and the Church use their body for sin. It receives more importance than is its due. It has its importance, but this rests in the Spirit.

Whatever wholly belongs to God in man, whatever God alone works in a soul's conversation with God, whatever cannot be defiled by sin: that is holy and adorable, not only venerable. God can and must be adored in his saints. Perhaps the disciples in their veneration for their Master might have progressed to this point . . . , but it would have been very difficult for the Lord to show it to them. The body of sin in each of them is like an obstacle to his making this visible to them in his own body (just as it is difficult for a husband to introduce his wife to his prayer if she has never learned to pray).

The Lord and Peter's Denial

In his dealings with the disciples, the Lord saw everything they did and everything that went on inside them. As he saw Nathanael under the fig tree, so he constantly saw into them with his supernatural perception. And while standing before the Sanhedrin, wholly occupied with what is happening here and now and concerned about assuming the attitude demanded by the Father, he is simultaneously with Peter and increasingly feels the mounting denial. He feels it is his body —that is the mystery of the Incarnation—the moment he feels Peter's body grow cold and rigid—as if through his denial Peter becomes a changed person, no longer belonging to him. Like a divorced man who after years stands once more beside his wife: he knows every secret of her body, but she is estranged from him, she belongs to somebody else. Certain characteristics that he once understood exactly have now become signals he can no longer read.

In this estrangement of Peter from him, in the offense it offers him, the Lord feels the coming Cross and the forsakenness and pain of sin. The sin of the one nearest to him somehow hits him harder than the many sins of all the rest.

A person who has committed a horrible deed almost without being aware of it can be overcome with dis-

gust and bitterness. This can also happen when someone close and a friend commits such a deed. It makes
one ''sick''. For the Lord, it is even worse, for the love
that bound him to Peter was stronger and purer than
any human friendship; this greater love shows up the
sin more heinously.

Each time Peter affirms ''I do not know this man'',
he rejects not only the Master personally but also his
whole teaching. He to whom this teaching had been
particularly entrusted appears not to know it at all. The
whole work of the Lord is presented as an illusion. Not
only his person, but also the whole New Covenant, the
Father's image erected in the world. In his first denial,
Peter knows nothing about it; in the second, tells himself he is rid of it; by the third, he becomes an enemy
knowing only himself.

The Church in the Lord
during the Passion

The Lord carries the Church in himself, a bit like a young man carries in himself the image of woman as he desires her to be: some aspects perhaps point to his mother, some to the girlfriends of his friends; others are imponderable; he has heard of them, wishes them to be; perhaps a whole range of ideal images melt together in him. He lives with this image and tries to acquire in himself something of what he learns, experiences and works for in view of it.

The Lord possesses his Mother's image in which to mold his Church; he has the Father's demand; he has his own will to redeem all men. As man he lives toward the realization of his ideal image; his intentions and plans are partly determined by it. The teachings and instructions he gives to people are ordered toward this Church he bears in himself: everything must become a unity that can become reality.

From heaven he knows the communion of saints; he wants to bring it to men on earth, and it should not suffer too much in the transition. It should become such that everyone is attracted by it, so many-sided that each one can be moved by it, and yet so unified that it can be taken back to heaven without difficulty.

During the Passion, the Lord in addition bridges the gap between ideal and reality, draws the opposition of sinners rejecting the ideal into himself in order to overcome it. Where Judas appears, where the apostles sleep, where all take to flight: there he begins to experience immediately in his own being the dichotomy caused by disobedience. When formerly he experienced human sin, the believers were closer to him than unbelievers, the lovers closer than those who reject. Now he himself moves into the center as the *object* of sin gathering all around him, and it is those closest to him who hurt him most. As sinners, they are more directly in opposition to him than the others. It is *he* whom Judas betrays, *he* whom Peter denies, *he* to whom the sleeping disciples are disobedient . . .

And more: he plans the Church to be his helpmate in the redemption. He wants her to be his gift to men as the place in the world that is as free from sin as possible. He wants to make her his spotless bride, as a grace continuously flowing from him, as the filial response to the eternal act of the Father's begetting. And now at the time when she is still within him, protected by him, in the act of becoming reality through him, he sees how sin accumulates around her. The first projection of the Church outside of him is a failure. For it is not as if he were to engender the Church outside of him at a later date while now she is still within him. He will always remain the center of the Church even though she is in the world. He will give her to the world as something of himself: which makes it all the more terrible that already now she looks as she does.

He is now at the same stage of his work with her as a researcher when he communicates his results to a small team of assistants and collaborators, so that they can begin to work with him, consult him, so that later, when he is no longer with them, they can continue the work without him according to his original design, always keeping his original intention before their eyes. What he in fact experiences at this stage is that his coworkers betray and deny him and leave him alone in his greatest difficulties.

Of course: as long as the Lord remained among his disciples as a mortal man, the integration planned looked different from what it does now when he suffers and hangs on the Cross. And the integration will enter a new stage again when, rising, he can point back to the Cross he suffered.

~

The Lord carries the Church in a way analogous to the human spirit having to carry along human drives and emotions, to the integration of the lower powers in the person into whole and fully human virtue. A perfectly pure person, for example, has drives. But they are well-ordered within his purity; purity is their safeguard. Perhaps he is in love with someone and his drives are set in motion; they build a bridge to the beloved other.

If the beloved is equally pure, the drives would all be well-ordered. But if he is inclined to sin, it could be that he lets his desire for a response become degenerate.

The Lord carries the Church as a man carries his drives in the shelter of purity. But when he delivers her to us, our responding drives can become degenerate. We make a harlot of the pure Church, a playground for our passions. By integrating the Church ever anew into himself, he purifies her ever anew. But since he made her for us, not himself, he gives her ever anew into our hands in a purified state, the purified Church to sinners as a Church striving ever anew for union.

The Church is the body of Christ: something that can be given. Christ the Incarnate One has a male body that is perfect. But to our incomprehension he does not marry. Why was he born with one sex if he does not need it? Why does he not combine both sexes? We cannot suppose that he does not value the good forces he has received in his body from the Father. He makes use of his endowments: for the creation of a visible fruit, the Church, the community of believers. The Church is his body in such a way that his physical body also finds its fulfillment in it. The acceptance of an individual human body is for him like a beginning for the birth of the Church and the fruitfulness particularly hers. It is not possible to separate the Church wholly from the Lord and place her beside him: she remains his body, although she is his bride. The key that explains it is the Eucharist. He surrenders his body in the Eucharist, in order to form the Church through the gathering together of what he has surrendered into unity. He has the power to lay down his life "and to take it up again". This remains a mystery of virginity; this also is one reason why priests should be celibate.

Passion and Fruitfulness

God said, the woman will bear children in pain, while the man must work in the sweat of his brow. The penalty for the first sin with its effects is passed on to the whole human race. The Son of God coming to redeem the world submits to the common destiny of man: he works, and he suffers pain. One could, of course, not say: he works in order to redeem man, and he suffers in order to redeem woman. He takes both on himself to redeem both; both together, and part of his labor is his pain, and part of his pain is his work. So he redeems the whole human race, men and women, as one.

But he works and suffers in love. It cannot be said that his love eases his work and softens his pain. His love perhaps makes his pain and work more differentiated, makes it stand out more. The whole punishment character of work and suffering is shown up through this love. In no one is the purpose of both so clear as in the Lord, the direct relationship to sin: he suffers birth pangs and labor for the redemption.

Pain belongs to the woman. But the woman's pain in giving birth is enclosed in the love for her husband and the love for her child. The Lord also lets his love enclose the pain. He, so to say, brackets it, subdues it, to show his love, to satisfy the expectation of the disciples, who, at the moment his body becomes a body of pain, want the Eucharist from him. (They are looking for a paschal lamb as only *he* can provide it.) In fulfilling this desire, he allows his love to cover the pain. Pain by itself without love is unfruitful. The Lord's Cross explains the meaning of the natural pains of childbearing. To bring children into the world is fruitfulness, redemption even more so. Both can be brought about only by a feminine self-giving in which love overcomes all suffering, pain and death. In some way the Lord suffers the Cross in place of Mary for woman. And the Church is crucified with the Lord, because he bears woman in himself in his suffering, Eve and Mary.

But he is also male, and it is his work to suffer on the Cross. The suffering is female, but the words he speaks from the Cross are male. And his most manly deed on the Cross is that in dying he hands his spirit back to the Father. He has the manly courage for this. He does not simply let the spirit escape; he gives it actively, thus completing his mission.

In the act of begetting, the man loses from his substance and gives to the woman the pain of the coming birth. The man is exhausted, and the woman goes into labor: the whole appears to be negative. But if it is done in love, the pain is surpassed by joy. The man loses in order to gain something out of all proportion. Both share the joys of being fruitful. Love transforms everything negative into something superabundantly positive.

Handed Over

There is the all-pervading sense of having to renounce something one is by nature entitled to. A certain physical well-being is a "normal" human condition, where the body is taken for granted, allowing the spirit a certain freedom of action. A whole series of normal sensations could be called to mind and renounced one by one. On the Cross the Lord's hand is pierced: *in retrospect* he realizes, it was a beautiful thing to have such a hand with which to do so many things. . . . It is the pain in addition to the fear that makes the lost member appear to be so great a good. In positive possession it appeared part of a whole—in its loss each part stands out by itself. His members are individually delivered over to those who mock, scourge, crucify him and put him to death.

Being thus handed over is another new experience, compared with a single abuse, for example, a box on the ear. To be handed over means for the prisoner, the captive, the one without rights, being handed over to all forms of possible ignominy: it almost does not matter which and how many are actually chosen.

The Lord has no possibility of distracting his mind. Neither has he the possibility of just waiting for things to happen: We shall see what they will pick out. His being handed over to sin opens every door; he can count on all concrete forms of humiliation and suffering; everything is possible. And the Lord carefully gathers the forms actually used; he feels them through to the bitter end. He offers himself expressly to them, so as not to let anything get lost. He does not flee from suffering into prayer to the Father, into the thought that it will soon be over, that everything is useful for the world. He opens himself to pain; he measures the offense to the Father by the offense offered to himself.

He is still wearing his garments, and there is some time still before the scourging. But he must not feel the protection afforded by the garments. And when reference is made to his statement that in three days he will raise the temple up again, everything concerning the temple is now applied to his body: the furnishings of the temple are his organs, which are "meant" and will "have their turn".

Here the "application of the senses" in the Ignatian Exercises takes on bitter seriousness. For the Lord, it means a total sensitivity of his body to the experience of pain, while being at the same time a praise and acknowledgment of this tool the Father thought of and created when he gave a body to Adam or to Christ or to all men. Acknowledgment of its marvellous structure, its harmony, its well-being, recognition of the individual senses and their mediating function. And because of this recognition, he now realizes how sin destroys this work of art from all sides, for through sin all of it can be used to inflict pain, humiliation, to remove it from the end for which the Father created it.

All this time the Lord also carries the body of the Church, giving it the possibility of feeling and suffering with him. The Eucharist is instituted before the Passion, so that the Church will never have to suffer for one minute without a eucharistic consciousness. The Lord as Bridegroom sends his bride, the Church, consciously into suffering. He takes her with him; he makes the decision to suffer for both together. He, so to speak, offers his own and the Church's hand to be pierced. As the Father sends him into suffering, so will he, when he thinks it right, send his Church into suffering, with the same suddenness and anguish, so that she can participate with him. But since he is the first who gives his body, and the only one who sets the example, the Church can never catch up with him. Even in her sufferings, she will be aware of his love, while he himself as the first of lovers no longer feels the Father's love. Here it becomes clear that his suffering embraces all the sufferings of the Church and that all her sufferings are graces of the following of Christ.

Judas' Repentance

There is a fear in the process of redemption that be-gins with the sufferer and spreads outward in concen-tric circles: he wants to flee from himself, beyond, but what flees there is his fear, which communicates itself to everything around it. The fear spreads, is flattened out like dough; and the sufferer is amazed: "Ah, even *that one* is fearful! Even *this one* is afraid! Even this thing is essentially an expression of fear!" And he no longer knows: Does he infect everything with fear, or does his own fear make him perceptive of the fear that already exists everywhere?

Judas' fear is something different. It is not he him-self that spreads fear to everything, but rather every-thing fits itself into his fear, oppresses him, invades the center of his fear; in everything he now perceives the expression of his sin. The borderlines become every-where effaced, for the things whose purpose is to give comfort and refreshment, to encourage new question-ing, have ceased to do anything but increase his fear. Perhaps they retain their justification to exist apart from fear. The friendship between the Lord and John could be something beautiful and right in itself. But I, Judas, experience it only as something that crushes me when I come near this reality, and the nearer I come, the more it does so. I find no fault now with this friendship, I who am an outcast. Formerly I would have envied it. Now it only crushes and condemns me.

And when every possibility of flight is cut off, and all things crush me the more, I can see with hindsight that I am myself the cause. I have betrayed. Fear now turns to remorse. It is the remorse of a wild animal that has risked running into the hunter's range. Remorse is born of a terrible fear for one's own life. It is the recognition that one has made a mistake, that one has miscalculated, taken a wrong step and made a wrong choice. Judas does not feel threatened exteriorly since his betrayal of the Lord, who is led to his death. But he has lost every inner support, every vestige of meaningfulness in his life, which had been much stronger than he believed. The word "sin" has almost wholly taken on the meaning of "mistake" for him. It is like a parody of the Lord's words: The first will be last. He had wanted to become free and is now in the trap. He wanted to get out of it all by the quickest way, and now he is inexorably caught.

A kind of demonic vision pursues him. The expression "vision" is not quite suitable, yet not false. A beautiful memory of a joyful event is woven from many individual traits; the memory does not retain the less positive ones. It transfigures reality. From a present joy one can also look backward: I hold a completed book in my hand and reflect on how it turned out and how much it comes up to my present expectation. It is the other way round with Judas. All the past receives its color from his present fear—the converse with the Lord and the disciples—even the most trifling things are seen in a demonic light. He feels a kind of greed for these images. With suspicion he pounces on everything in case he can get still more out of them. Everywhere he beholds the signs of betrayal; in everything he sees his destiny prefigured, everything points toward it; he projects the signs of malice into the infinitesimal moments, as if he had always already been mixing poison for himself. This increases his fear and his "repentance". He cannot be satisfied with the fact of his betrayal; he must touch on everything and make it evil. He sees himself as one who has acted for the devil. And when in his thoughts he tries to undo something he has done, not to sell the Lord on *this* occasion, not to say the evil word on *that* occasion, and hold back from the path of betrayal: he sees everywhere that it is too late. There already, on that other occasion, everywhere he sees: I have always with unremitting consistency taken the part of opponent.

He is far removed from Christian repentance. But he presents an absolutely exact example of a certain kind of repentance encountered frequently in confessionals: repentance for one's own sake. It is not sin itself that is heinous to me but its consequences for me. So I am looking for a way out of my present unbearable situation in the priest's words. For Judas, the betrayal contained the hope of freeing himself from the Lord, of ceasing to have a master over himself. And now he "repents'' because he did not succeed in liberating himself. His ''confession'' (his words to the Jews in the temple are a kind of confession) is the sign that he seeks a way out. He cannot confess to the Lord himself; for he does not want to compromise himself by seeking him out in his present situation as prisoner. So he passes his guilt on to his employers. In saying that he no longer stands by his deed, he is rejected by them also. Nevertheless there is a certain *completeness* in his deed and repentance. Were he to go to the Lord, this completeness would break down; he would begin to maneuver. He cannot be excused on the grounds that the sacrament of confession has not yet been instituted. He knows the Our Father; he knows that God forgives sin. But he does not go to God.

The end is a heavy barrage. He runs to his death as someone haunted. He absolutely abhors his body. Everything he sees of himself fills him with disgust. He commits his body and spirit to destruction. Fear presses on him from outside and enters into his inner center. He dies like a fortress surrounded on all sides and stormed, blasting itself into the air.

King of the Jews
(*Dictated in a state of "hell"*)

Adrienne: Is it necessary? (I: What?) A. To whom am I talking? Do you know saints? What is the difference between a saint with a mission and any other man? (I: He has been sent.) A: And this mission is anchored in heaven; it is not floating in the air . . . Can you imagine a saint on earth whom you may meet tomorrow? What is he doing? He can be a teacher or a doctor, for example . . . You become aware of him and have the impression he could be a saint. You meet other teachers who tell you things about him. He fulfills his task exceedingly well . . . He has a good influence on his students, though he must also know some who fail . . . Among his colleagues he is collegial, helps wherever he can; no human question leaves him insensitive. What do you do with such a person? (I: ?) A. He is genuine, a good man. Then you hear about another, a Catholic teacher who often goes to church, fasts often, prays and keeps vigils, who makes retreats, and again there is the question: Is he a saint? This is on another level. A man who does these things must have been touched by something . . . You do not hear more. There is a sort of *nihil obstat* with regard to his holiness. The question remains open. Besides the belonging to the world of the first one, you have found in the second a belonging to the Church. Does he also belong to heaven? If nothing unforeseen happens, you will learn *after his death* whether he was a saint. Maybe the Church will recognize him as one who will have his special place in heaven. Once he has a permanent position there, he will be asked to care for the needs of the Church.

(She sees somebody, smiles): I don't know whether he will understand. I don't understand myself either . . . The Lord stood in front of Pilate. His human identity is established. Are you the King of the Jews? Behind this lies the unspoken question: Are you the son of Mary and Joseph? His human identity is not questioned. He could still be King of the Jews if the Jews had elected him. But no: He is King of the Jews because of his heavenly task, his divine mission. It belongs to his divinity to be at the same time also King of this people. This title has its place somewhere between his Godhead and his manhood. (She takes her shoes off.) That is my human foot, and that is my divine foot. And you watch me walk, the way I put one foot before the other, how my feet relate to each other. And suddenly you recognize from them the third: "King of the Jews". It is a *tertium; tertium entis,* not *comparationis.* It is the Lord's being, uniting his divinity and his humanity in a form recognizable to the Jews. The *tertium entis* is that which unites and fuses the other two kinds of being in a form that is comprehensible to me. If the expression *tertium entis* sounds dangerous, one could say: *unitas entis,* or the *visible ens* or *entis* . . . Here could be an open access for the Jews to the recognition of the *ens invisibile*.

The saint also has something of such a *tertium ens*. One cannot disturb or interrupt him in what he is. I could perhaps interrupt the Catholic teacher in an occupation but not in his deeper being where his natural and his supernatural being is united. It is obvious that there is no contradiction for him in being a teacher and a saint. The proofs of his holiness are recognizable for you in a *third area;* this area would contain what I can see that bears the marks of the two other areas. You may come upon him reading, and he does not hear you and goes on reading: he reads like an ordinary human being and like a saint, which means, one who has a vision of heaven, not necessarily with his eyes. And when he afterward explains to you what he was reading, you will receive a new insight into his holiness.

The evidence of the Lord's holiness could be found much more quickly and surely. It is grasped in the term "King of the Jews". There must exist for the recognition of holiness an expression that mediates both levels.

One could also point to the miracles. Miracles are no magic. Miracles are the evident side of holiness. But even the hidden side of holiness can become evident. As a human being, that person is not commonplace. He will rather try to understand and live his human life as part of his mission. That is one piece of evidence, a point to keep in mind. In the Lord the living for his mission points to the "King of the Jews".

It is understandable that saints recognize one another more quickly: through this *tertium entis* that each one divines in himself without recognizing himself as a saint. But he can recognize it in the other.

Are you a theologian? Are you trying to live your theology? Then you have a standpoint. You have something that makes you understand holiness. And from this point you could form a judgment of men, their ordinariness or possible holiness. This fits into it, that does not, and that is even more unsuitable.

"King of the Jews." The Lord knows what this is. The Jews ought to know it. Pilate could come to know it.

Pilate

From whatever side you approach him, you cannot put him into a category. He does not want evil. He uses a yardstick by which to judge the Lord; this yardstick is not totally wrong; he comes to the conclusion that the Lord is allright, there is nothing to find fault with. But exactly here he gets stuck. This is so because no one can approach the Lord with a yardstick. Instead of measuring, he would need to believe. One could try to excuse him; where should he suddenly find faith? But there are the disciples: their encounter with the Lord was sufficient to awaken the faith to which they were open. Pilate fits neither into faith nor into community. He isolates himself by his way of measuring. He does not even wholly fit into the words: "Anyone who is not for me, is against me." For in some way he is for the Lord.

He does not fit into any "state of life"; he makes no election that commits him for life. He has married, so to say, without entering into partnership. He is a bachelor. The wife he chose makes his loneliness more acute. He *could* be useful to the Lord, but in the place where he is he is useless.

His objectivity is such that it could indicate the place where the Church would stand. For the disciples have disappeared; the Jews only hate. He gathers to his ob-

jective stance the Yes of the absent disciples and the
No of the present Pharisees. His objectivity beyond
all parties could be an ecclesial objectivity. But since
it is not the objectivity of faith, he cannot communicate with the Lord from his objective standpoint.
This is the level where the majority in the Church
take their position. Pilate, who is no Christian, has
become in this the most influential model for Christians. How many repeat his words: "I find no guilt in
this man." The Lord is allright as he is. Uncommitted
well-wishing, leaving the responsibility to the Church's
representatives. These nonparticipants undermine the
Church more thoroughly than her enemies. An unbe-
liever who sees what the Lord really means to these
Christians will find it almost impossible to make a distinction between this Church and the Lord. The Lord
is the one in whom this sort of Christians believe. Real
Judas-figures are rarer in the Church than these benev-
olent, nonengaged Pilate-natures.

Pilate's Wife (Mt 27:19)

The loneliness of this woman is great. She is much more decisive and alive than her husband; she does not have the inhibitions his office imposes on him. She has a strange objectivity, flowing from her subjectivity. She has suffered for his sake, has felt deeply disturbed on his behalf and felt all the time: her state has to do with him. The uneasiness leads her to the conclusion: He must be a just man. It is not the justice of the Lord himself that forces this conclusion on her but her strange disquiet. She comes upon the Lord in her suffering yet does not find a relationship to him. She is aware of a possible relationship, a negative one, something that must not happen: it increases her isolation. When the disciples suffer something for the Lord, then it is within their belonging to him and in love, and this love grows through it. With her it is the reverse, for she has no share in faith and no communion with the Lord. He is not one of those she has access to. He is a prisoner. In a double way: the prisoner of the judge and the prisoner of the faith he represents and gives. Even in relation to her husband, she becomes more and more lonely: even though she knows that he must have nothing to do with this just man, they do not find one another on any level. She has to interrupt his official duty to tell him the private thing she has experienced; it is a warning, not a trusting communication. And she does not get to him directly but indirectly, not to the spouse but to the judge. She becomes estranged also from the people who will decide otherwise. This is an experience of suffering in an isolated solitude, not reaching a real com-passion, for faith is lacking and so the access to it. The woman reminds one of people on the outside, who are touched but do not take the step into faith for one reason or another.

Barabbas

He has committed murder, very well. More important is that he knows he has become famous through his deed. He attracts a kind of interest, is a sensation for the people. He knows it; he laps it up and suns himself in his notoriety. If someone were suddenly to ask him: If you are set free, would you commit murder again? He would have to say: I do not know. I know only one thing: I want to attract more attention. If what I did is sufficient for this, I need not trouble myself further. This is a quite specific sin. He did not murder to gain popularity. But what has resulted from it has now become indispensable to him. Through his heinous deed he has become somebody great, feared as much as loved. He provides entertainment for the crowd. Now that the crowd has to choose between him and Christ, it does not make a choice between good and evil, grace and sin; it merely chooses the most sensational. The crowd goes for the greater excitement without taking account of the quality of what is offered. It chooses the greater entertainment.

This seems to be less evil than choosing between good and evil, but it is more depraved. For the people make no spiritual choice at all and do not penetrate to a greater depth. The Jewish people is not the Church. But they are doing something that will recur frequently in the Church: thinking and coming to conclusions that

have nothing to do with faith, ignoring the contrast between good and evil.

The Lord is much more moved by Pilate than by
Barabbas. The seeming objectivity of Pilate touches
him more than the subjective stance of Barabbas. It is
a deep humiliation for him that a thug should be pre-
ferred to him. But it is even more humiliating to stand
in front of Pilate. Pilate has the whole of his humiliation in his hand. It is Pilate who brings this confrontation with Barabbas about. And he does it from apparent
objectivity, pretended friendliness for the Lord and the
people. Barabbas is somebody who could stand for any
scoundrel: the most painful part is the fact that Pilate
positively finds no guilt in the Lord but that this does
not lead him to conversion.

Sin everywhere: the people want their pleasure; Barabbas boasts of his sin; Pilate does not take responsibility. Even piety has sin for its center here. As if every
prayer came out of sin, circling around sin instead of
God. Prayer can be a kind of security psychosis: Who
knows what may happen if I do not pray? Or one's
eyes can be riveted on sin, not knowing yet whether
one will commit it or not. Or in the form of watching for it because it attracts me, but not having the
courage and strength to commit it. Prayer can be the
place where I occupy myself with sin and even lust after it. The people choose entertainment, as the Christian also often does in prayer . . . while making a thousand excuses. Barabbas enjoys himself. Pilate wants to
be left in peace.

The People's Call
and the Call of God

Adam was the first to be chosen by God, chosen to be father of all mankind. Later God chooses numerous others, somehow to Adam's measure. He gives them a similar chance; they are tainted with original sin, which impairs this chance, but they also have a certain knowledge and experience of sin, which increases their chance of avoiding evil. The Father sent the chosen ones of the Old Testament, as patriarchs and prophets, analogous to Adam. For Adam, too, received the word of God as a prophet; but there was as yet only Eve to whom to transmit it.

In the Son's Incarnation, the Father gains another measure. For the election, he uses the measure of Adam; for the mission, that of the Son. The missions of the elect are all included in the all-embracing mission of the Son. In this the chosen ones of the New Covenant are privileged above those of the Old: they need to go back, not to Adam, who failed, but instead to the mission of the Son, who fulfilled it perfectly.

The incarnate Son is chosen by the Father. Uniquely chosen. For the Father, there is no one comparable to him. But within his mission other missions are possible.

Pilate gives the people a choice between Barabbas and Christ. The people choose Barabbas, rejecting Christ. They do not choose according to the mind of the Father, for whom every choice is one included in Christ. The Father's call is the expression of the chosen one's remaining in him. The people's call expresses their assimilation of their chosen one into themselves. The more differentiated and exposed a mission, the surer and stronger is the abiding in God, the more so the farther away one is sent. And also: the more differentiated a mission is, the more personal and clearly defined is its form. When the people choose someone, they cannot guarantee his remaining theirs, and they have no insight into the mission they bestow. They choose without choosing.

Pilate offers the choice: Christ or Barabbas. But the Father has already chosen: an ultimate, irrevocable choice. So he does not allow the mission of the Son he has sent to be crossed or weakened by any other authority. Were the people to choose Christ, the way of the Lord's suffering would be interrupted. So the choice offered to the people by Pilate can only be the parody of a choice. The sinful people cannot choose what God chooses. For this they would have to reject Pilate's alternative and choose Christ, and within Christ Barabbas.

At the moment it becomes clear how the people will choose, the question of choice arises with new urgency in the Father. From now on the Father no longer chooses according to Adam's measure but solely according to the mission of the Son. And we now have to choose between Christ and ourselves. Between what belongs to the Father and what belongs to the sinful creature. We (as Adam's children) can choose ourselves in no other way than as included in Christ.

Until now in the Gospel only individuals had been called to choose: the choice of the disciples, the high priests, the rich young man . . . Here for the first time the people is asked to choose. This people is composed of a crowd of imprisoned subjects: imprisoned in themselves and in the great mass of the others. Barabbas represents what is earthly and sinful; Christ, what is divine. In choosing Barabbas, one need not renounce anything. God sees in the people how humanity will choose. Whoever chooses the Lord chooses the life of the Lord and death for himself. Whoever chooses Barabbas chooses his own life—and the Lord's death. At the moment, however, when the Son goes to his death, the gift resulting from his suffering is due to him from the Father: he, the Father, will henceforth choose men within the mission of the Son. We are being chosen in communion with the Son's mission.

It is the moment when the Lord is rejected by all, the moment of his absolute loneliness. And it is here that a community at the heart of Christian missions begins: at the moment of loneliness. Because the people in its choice excludes life, the Father will from now on only choose inclusively: all living missions in the dying Son.

Simon of Cyrene

Simon is not a man of prayer. But he is taken into service when the Lord is at the end of his strength: his strength as God and as man to carry these cross-beams seems to fail. His repeated falls under the burden and the failure of his strength manifest that his bodily forces are those of the average man of his age. His spirit will suffer far beyond human capacity, but no possibility exists for his spiritual strength to stretch his bodily strength indefinitely. It is late when he will succumb, but succumb he will.

For Simon, who is healthy and strong, not weakened by suffering, it is not hard to help in the carrying. The burden is the same. For the God-man it has become unbearable, but this average man is not overtaxed by it. Simon does it for the Lord who gave the commandment of love of neighbor: in fulfilling this commandment, his action is reckoned to him as an act of faith in the Lord. And since faith is expressed in prayer, his action is counted as living faith, as prayer. Whether he knows it or not, what he *does* is in effect to offer his strength to Christ.

The Father sees the loss of strength of his incarnate Son. He also sees him as he would see one of his creatures. He sends him help in the form of a fellow man. And since the Son suffers to redeem men, he sends him one of those to be redeemed and draws this one into the divine life of prayer because of the help offered to the Son.

The Holy Spirit, who is totally devoted to the work of the Incarnation of the Son and his task on earth, to whom the Father and the Son had entrusted the hour of the birth and so the task of overshadowing and who keeps to the hour fixed by the Father for the Son's death: this Holy Spirit takes care that the Son does not die from exhaustion before his time but receives the necessary assistance to help him reach the Father's hour, which is also the Son's. He inspires Simon, not yet a believer, not to refuse giving help, and through this act the Holy Spirit can take possession also of his soul.

Cross and Confession

Adrienne sees the Cross and on it the sins that by freely willed decision have not been confessed. These are sins that have been omitted from confession or expressed in such a way as to say something different from the sin one does not want to mention. There are also confessors who are in a hurry and who one knows by experience will cut the confession short after a few things have been said. One also can confess in such a way that the sin not confessed is somehow "included". There are also the many confessions that are no longer taken seriously. All this has filled the previous night with hours of anguish for Adrienne.

Not to take confession seriously is not to take one's Christian life seriously. Sooner or later one will be moving out of the ambience of the Catholic Church into heresy or unbelief. It is possible to create for oneself with one's remaining strength a new center from one's most vital point, which is no longer at rights, which will satisfy one's surroundings if not oneself. A certain feeling for propriety can lead to this solution.

I do not want to confess my sin: confession appears to me oppressive and humiliating. This light makes my whole life look false. So away from the sphere of the confessional! And this in order to begin a decent life anew from here. To move away from confession means of necessity: to move away from the Lord. As long as I went to confession, I knew the Lord's joy; I also knew how the covering up of my sin saddened him. It blocks for me the access to his life, to his way of thinking. Without confession we cannot accompany the Lord. We can perhaps adore and admire him from afar but not walk with him side by side. If in a friendship one partner is in the same mood day after day, without any emotional change, this would be perfectly boring for the other. So it is with the sublime image of Christ many Protestants have. Through confession, the Lord creates a tension in our relationship with him, which, while distancing us from himself, draws us at the same time closer to him. We are most deeply aware of his greatness when he draws us close to himself in absolution.

Mary certainly does not need confession to be drawn closer to the Lord. But in seeing him taking sin on himself even before the Cross, forgiving, teaching, healing and taking human weakness on himself, she feels still more attracted to him and is more ready than before to carry with him. She becomes more deeply aware that the real and difficult accompaniment of the Lord consists in bearing sin with him. She is drawn closer to her Son through what is most foreign to her. She has to learn to feel closest to him when something separates them absolutely: sin. The more this shocks her, the more pliable she becomes. By resisting this terrible thing, her surrender receives a new nuance. It is as if she had to flee from sin in shock and fear, and in this movement away she is newly accepted by the Son. And she cannot flee anywhere but to the Son in his suffering. The more she desires to flee from the sin he carries, the nearer she comes to him who cannot be separated from it. It is now that she experiences the whole *strength* of his love. For she is not fleeing from him but from the sin that lies on him; he does not keep her back, because she does not flee from him; he keeps her back only insofar as he is one with the sin from which she flees. And while she is seeking him on the long roundabout way of flight, he has never for a moment let go of her hand.

On the Cross
(*Dictated in a state of "hell"*)

Adrienne: I have been commissioned to share in the carrying of the Cross from within. It is your task to understand. (*She takes off her watch.*) It is too heavy. I must have my hands free. Otherwise one cannot feel the wood. And I am not allowed to cry out. The wages of sin is death. The death on the Cross now represents this wage. Death is the reward and result of my sin. Every sin leads to death. But who will see the connection? Who has any idea how much of what is positive is destroyed in men through sin? Through theft perhaps one's whole attitude to honesty has died long before one dies. One's physical death contains also the trace of this earlier death. There are deaths that can be the direct result of sin: death from syphilis, for example. It can also happen that one dies a good death while becoming aware of what sin has already killed long before. The person who is already dead has to die once more in order to prepare himself for the resurrection.

(*She extends her arms.*) Now the crown of thorns is put in place; now the nails are hammered in, and with every blow sins are hammered into the soul and body of the Lord. The crown is formed from existing sins, those I intend to commit or those I am not finished with. The nails are formed of those of the past, the forgotten ones, those one no longer wishes to acknowledge or remember. (*She sighs*.) Ah, and he made up for it all. For everything, everything. For everyone.

When the nails penetrate, they burst into the body of Christ all at once. Imagine that all the sins of my whole life, even those of mere thought, become present and penetrate into me through my hands and feet. They penetrate through an unimaginably painful recognition. And the sins of the crown do not penetrate but make their mark. And the more painful it is and the more tired one is, so much the more still follows after. (*A. is wholly exhausted, closes her eyes.*) Don't you see it?

This monstrous shame. Now one has to receive for *every* sin the wage that is called death. Imagine someone who would want to make reparation in his living flesh for everything, for example, for every murder. Every murderous intention as well. He would become mincemeat. Even taking on just one small category of sin would already be totally unthinkable. But the Lord bears all sins and, so, all the kinds of death one could think of. And he bears it not as victim, as blows from without; he does not merely offer his body but hands over his whole being. He bears every sin from within as if he himself had committed it, with all its shame. A shame that now does not admit of repentance. Repentance and confession belong together in a unity that originates from the Cross, beyond the

Cross. On the Cross, the Lord only reaches the insight into the heinousness of sin.

(*She looks up to the Cross*.) Every time one thinks one is about to die, one is disappointed, because the death of sin is timeless. It is a state of being, a mirrored image of being sinful. (*She whispers:*) Is it not possible to cover up this shame?

What can one do? Is this the Father's will? "Into your hands I commend my spirit": Do you know what this means? The Lord gives his whole innocent spirit to the Father and keeps only our own sinful spirit back for himself. In this way he can carry sin as if he himself had committed it. The spirit in which he carries it can no longer be identified as "clean" or "unclean". He commits no sin, but when the crown of thorns is pressed on his head, he welcomes sins as his own property into himself, without his pure spirit losing anything of its purity. But in a way as if he were about to commit all sins.

Now it is I whose sins he carries. I have committed them all. Have I now to go where I deserve to go? I deserve hell. I cannot remain here. If someone had struck me a mortal wound, he would not remain standing in a corner to watch me slowly dying . . . If I only knew what to do . . . Are you not able to help me, to help him? Have you nothing with which to cover me?

Should I pray? That the Father forgives us? How can that be possible since I am busy murdering his child? Can the Father forgive us while we are all doing this?

But, Father, you must have mercy now on your Son. And are you not forced to have mercy on us also? Between the Son and us there is no longer a separation. Since the Son is right in the midst of our sin, as its center, the Father can have mercy on him only by passing through our sin.

This Son who has handed over his divinity, his whole spirit to the Father, in order to be only man, is that man who lived without experiencing sin otherwise than in others. But because he now wants to be only the Son of Man, the exemplar of man, he has to experience every sin in the same way men *would* if . . .

There is nothing ever so intimate that does not now undergo profanation. Every possible form of love is wounded in every possible way. And the Son has here to discover himself with his pure soul: in the midst of the most secret malice. As if someone finds himself doing what he had sworn to himself he would never do. The Son feels the same abhorrence for every sin, but he does not repel it as something foreign; he allows it to settle on himself. There is no way of deadening the impact. One sin more or less does not matter to a sinner; he would not mind taking on one for another person occasionally. His conscience is blunted. But the Lord feels every sin with his whole soul and body. In his death he dies all deaths. He leaves no sin behind as something finished with. Each one causes his death. The sin that is intended, the sin that is willed, the sin committed, everything always up to the limit where repentance begins, up to total abhorrence. And by going the way of terrible, perfect recognition (by means of his purity) he opens for us the way to repentance and confession. He himself is now unable to confess; he has no time left. Everything clashes so monstrously together that in grasping one thing, he always grasps everything else with it.

And all this in obedience! What can that mean: "Into your hands I commend my spirit"? (*A. sinks into a kind of faint. She whispers:*) There are still more parts that have to die . . . I thirst. (*She licks her lips, then she no longer moves. She calls my name in a hardly audible fashion.*) Adieu.

Wood of the Cross

In the wood of the Cross the Lord sees the tree and human work united. Men must work because they have sinned, and so they lay the curse of their own sin into their work; they hammer the Cross together in order to nail him who brings salvation to it.

A. sees the Lord repeatedly attempting to fit his body to the Cross (and she has to do it with him). It is like trying on a dress to make it fit. "This now" is how the wood of the Cross feels on the naked skin, and "this" is how the horizontal beam is felt by arms and hands, and "this" what the vertical beam feels like on the whole length of the back . . . A kind of foretaste. Like someone who knows that he will die at the stake will hold a lighted match to his skin for a moment, in order to have a foretaste.

∼

It is clear that Christ had to become a carpenter, for he had to cut down the tree of knowledge. Like the first Adam, he as second Adam had also to deal with a tree. The first Adam had to do with the fruit; by eating it he made the tree unfruitful. The second Adam has to cope with the dead tree. During the years of his contemplation, he takes the dead material of the felled tree and makes it his life's work. The wood becomes something like his obligatory prayer of the office; it structures his contemplative day. He has to rededicate the tree desecrated by the eating of the apple so that it can become the Cross.

Adam as soul and body had committed a sin of soul and body; his soul drew his body into sin, for he ate the apple with his body. He was driven out of paradise for this, but the odium was left on the tree. It is Christ who has to purify Adam in soul and body and to restore the tree to its place. During his contemplative years, he "trains" his human soul and body for the work of redemption. Through his professional work he in a way also "trains" the tree for himself. When one sees with what tenderness he dies on the wood, one understands what its rehabilitation means. The tree of the Cross was found worthy to carry the Lord and to experience its own death as a tree as part of the Lord's death. The tree dies to sin at the moment when the Lord inflicts death on the sin in us.

The Body on Holy Saturday
(*Dictated in a state of "hell"*)

(*A. is speaking with someone:*) At what beginning? . . .
He will never understand it. There are two beginnings.
There is the first beginning, God, let us say, the Father,
and in the beginning was the Word. The beginning of
the Father, the Word, the Spirit: these are beginnings
we cannot trace back, because it is the beginning per
se. And this absolute beginning is also absolute eternity, eternal duration. It is as unsearchable as the end
of eternal time. It will forever be incomprehensible to
us that there is a beginning in the eternal. All God's ut-
terances participate in his triune eternity: they are not
limited to space or time. And so the reasons for God's
manifestation of himself to us are inscrutable.

Then God sets a new beginning by creating the
world. This beginning is one of time, it has a "place",
a why, a clearly definable life. (I don't understand anything of it, and it is a great labor for me.) Men are
placed into this new beginning, with their span of life,
their form, their boundaries. These boundaries are now
what is important. But these boundaries are such that
they are not awkward for the creature, as long as there
is no sin. To be a creature is *not a bad thing* even though
it implies limitation. As long as creatures are in God,

their actions are determined by the action of God. The beginnings they make, the actions they perform, are within the sphere of God's eternal will, can be compared to him and are not opposed to him. And their finite form, their limitations, do not contradict God's infinity. Their time can be easily understood and fitted into the eternal time of God.

Only sin makes the limitations stand out: a harsh contrast, in contradiction to eternity. Time becomes the opposite of God's timelessness, the space and place of his all-pervading presence, the limited form contradicts God's boundlessness. Everything that exists becomes separated, limited, hampered. Man's deeds are turned against God's deeds. Everyone becomes incredibly *lonely,* because everywhere he comes up against his own limitations.

Then the Son becomes incarnate. He assumes the boundaries and measures of a body and, to a large degree, the human way of acting in a fallen world. But because he does in all things the Father's will, he does not come across his limitations, as Adam in paradise did not either. We alone are constantly hampered by these limitations, because he carries our sin, because he has come to save us, and because we do not look at him with the eyes of the redeemed but are still to be redeemed.

But since he became an individual while being God, he opens the way back to God for us individuals. And he seeks to open to eternal time everything that binds us to time. By taking our limits on himself, he also explodes them. He does this through the Cross, in which he takes on the experience of our separateness, our dependence on others, our powerlessness. But while these limits become unbearable for him on the Cross, he gives his body to all who are his own. In a dispensation that leads to the Father. He gives them his limited body in a new eucharistic boundlessness, so that he himself can bear the Cross and die on it as a mere man.

It is an exchange. He gives us his substance eucharistically in an eternal openness to the Father, Son and Spirit; it is *for this* he takes our sins upon himself. In order to do this more and more, he constantly engenders the Church. The craftiness of our refusals is increasingly overcome by the cunning of his love.

. . . Which of the Fathers has written this . . . transmission, substitution? . . . Did I have another life before this? (I: Why?) She: Because I know these Fathers. I have merely forgotten their names. I know them as a doctor knows the people lying in hospital beds. (I: Hilary? Athanasius?) She: I think it is Hilary . . . He has a certain feeling for love . . . A robust physique . . . Adrienne should be shown a text by Hilary when she returns . . . Why Ignatius? What a mixture! When did A. live? (I: 1948.) She: What is the year now? It could be the year 0 or just as well the year 3000 . . . But I am not sure whether the past is not the future . . . When Ignatius says: Give Adrienne a text from Hilary, he is saying from his sixteenth century that the fourth century should be shown to the twentieth. This is probably the mark of eternal time . . . Is that enough for you? Do you want to ask something?

All this turns around the limits of our bodies, our actions and intentions in this world. And our human plans seen as destiny, and the plans of God as providence.

Let us say I am a man who has three sons. They are still immature; I cannot speak to them. I see their inclinations, their behavior at home and at play, as boys aged six, eight, or ten years. The eldest boy would be fit to become a country doctor in the village; my income is enough to let him take this road. According to human thinking, this could happen. The second delights in nature, is gifted for agriculture; I plan for him to go to an agricultural college; I send him into the country to farmers so that he may learn and feel in his blood how young farmers feel . . . And my third son looks a bit like a poet, sensitive, aesthetic in his feelings; whatever he sees and thinks he has to express in a beautiful form. So I plan to show him beautiful things and educate him so that he will later have the possibility of becoming a poet or artist. These are reasonable human plans. It can happen that providence will thwart them all one day, and everything may look different, and one has to begin to plan all over again.

If we were not sinners, our plans would be made within the plans of God, and our course of action would be the outcome of God's action. If you like, my make-up, my horoscope, are tied to my body; they participate in its imperfection. This body bears above all one mark: it is a fallen body. The limitations that now stand out so starkly would have been of no consequence if there had been no sin; they would always have been open to God's boundlessness.

In *hell* the Lord's bodily state becomes very different from what it was in life. (I: What is it like?) She: It is difficult to say; one cannot express in words all that one feels. It is something like this: in life, the Son of Man feels and experiences in his body wherever godlessness is hidden, be it in individual people with whom he deals or in the surrounding atmosphere. The power of evil appears to him as enmity with God. In hell, he experiences the power of evil, not in its relationship with God, but as a quality in itself. As that which makes a work of the devil to be such. God is so far distant from hell that it would be almost a consolation to know that this particular thing is directed *against him*. He could be defined in relation to something. But now the quality of evil is not related to anything.

(I: How is this felt in the body?) She: As if the body had the possibility of existing without being related to God. As if it could be complete and cut off from everything, as sin is here. It is as if the body received so many possibilities of evil that the possibilities for good are nullified. (I: How can the Lord experience this?) She: *Because he has been robbed of his Eucharist.*

The Cross lies behind him and is no longer relevant.
And his physical being with its striving seems at this
moment left behind with men in the Eucharist, in the
same way as his martyred body has been left behind on
the Cross. Whatever united him with God the Father
and with mankind, everything horizontal and vertical,
has been left behind. Something like this: in the world,
I eat when I am hungry and dress myself when I am
cold. In hell, however, when I accompany the Lord
on Holy Saturday, I no longer know: Will I be hungry? Will I be thirsty? Must I dress up? Eat? Or must
I withdraw completely into myself? Be body to such a
degree that I no longer know the needs and questions
concerning them . . . I would like to go home now.
(I fetch her back with a prayer.)